736·2

30p

6206·

HAND LAPIDARY CRAFT

9.50

HAND LAPIDARY CRAFT

Graham Geldart

B T Batsford Ltd London

To I. J. F and P.

Colour photographs by René Sudan

© Graham Geldart 1980
First published 1980

ISBN 0 7134 1536 3

Filmset by Willmer Brothers Limited
Birkenhead, Merseyside
Printed by The Anchor Press Limited
Tiptree, Essex

for the publishers B T Batsford Limited
4 Fitzhardinge Street, London W1H 0AH

CONTENTS

To every thing there is a season, and a time
  to every purpose under the heaven:
A time to cast away stones, and a time to
  gather stones together;
. . . I perceive that there is nothing better,
  than that a man should rejoice in his own works . . .

Ecclesiastes 3.1; 3.5; 3.22

INTRODUCTION

What is the point of working stones by hand when there is a whole range of machines on the market specially designed for the use of amateurs? The point is to bring a not very well known but fascinating hobby within reach of masses of people, especially boys and girls, who may think that machines are an absolute necessity for practising the lapidary craft.

Amateur craftsmen working in wood make beautiful things with hand tools; they do not need circular saws or planing machines because they do not start off with tree trunks. In the same way it is now possible to buy minerals which have already been processed from their original state, cut into convenient sized slices for making cabochons or pre-formed ready for faceting. (A glossary of terms which make up the technical vocabulary of lapidaries will be found at the end of the book.) As the hobby grows more popular, and the demand from the public increases, there will be better selections of these prepared pieces and more places where they can be bought. At the present time there should be little difficulty for an amateur lapidary to find suitable material and buy it by mail order from the suppliers who advertise in lapidary magazines, if there is no shop nearby.

Hand work can also enable groups of workers, either in schools or in lapidary clubs, to take advantage of a limited number of machines. For example, an hour or so spent working on a trim saw and grinding wheel can produce enough pre-forms to supply a small class of faceters using hand units; or blanks can be prepared for making cabochons at home on a hand wheel. In this way those who do not have a machine in their homes can still take up lapidary work and use their hands to produce gemstones of real value.

The various finished stones described here can all be produced by hand using extremely simple apparatus which can be made with a minimum of skill and with very few tools. It is quite astonishing what beautiful results can be obtained from such elementary equipment, but they will not be achieved without a fair amount of patience and attention to detail.

The chapters are arranged to lead a complete beginner step by step from polishing a simple pebble to faceting a standard brilliant, but there are a few unorthodox ways of working which may appeal to experienced lapidaries. There is no need to start at the beginning and follow the whole programme, so anybody who is not in the least interested in pebbles or cabochons but wants to start faceting immediately can do so. There is no obvious reason for the traditional habit of learning to cut cabochons before becoming a faceter, but you cannot facet if you do not know how to dop a stone properly, and the work will be much easier if you have first had some practice in flat lapping.

There are obvious drawbacks to working by hand, the chief one being the impossibility of sawing hard stones without a power-driven diamond sawblade. In addition, grinding by muscle power is a slow process which becomes tedious after a time, so it must be done in small doses. On the other hand a start can be made for a trifling cost, and if the hobby is abandoned no harm has been done. Alternatively the enthusiast who has discovered the joys of a new hobby and has acquired a certain degree of skill will be much better equipped when it comes to choosing more sophisticated apparatus.

Perhaps the most important point of all is that lapidary work pursued as a hobby, and not as a means to earn money, is an absorbing pastime and a gateway to a whole range of new interests in subjects like mineralogy, geology, gemmology, jewellery, palaeontology etc, all of which have something to do with stones.

Practical considerations

'Whenever I come across a book which tells me how to do things I always feel a complete fool because I don't understand half the things people take for granted.' The lady who made this remark was no doubt familiar with the kind of cookery book which begins 'make a roux' but does not say how it is done. The aim of this book is to describe in detail exactly what needs to be done and to supplement the information with illustrations. It may be a comfort to know that all the apparatus needed has been designed, put together and tested by the author to make quite sure that it works, so if the instructions are followed carefully there is every reason to expect excellent results, even without previous experience.

The dictionary definition of a lapidary is 'an artificer who cuts, polishes or engraves precious stones'. What distinguishes a lapidary from other workers in stone such as masons and sculptors, apart from the preciousness of his stone, is that the others can cut or carve their material with metal tools, whereas the lapidary is mostly concerned with stone which is so hard that no metal can make any impression on it.

This is the reason why the art of the lapidary has always been a closely guarded secret among a few professionals who passed on their skill to a restricted number of followers. Recent developments in synthetic abrasives and diamond-impregnated tools have rendered some traditional practices obsolete, and have enabled amateurs to start working in this extremely interesting field which was formerly closed to them. This trend started in the United States some thirty years ago, and it is now developing rapidly in Europe as manufacturers cater for a growing market in machinery and more shops are stocking minerals and essential lapidary supplies.

The first thing to do is to find one of these shops, because they are the only ones where you can buy the grits and polishing powders which are absolutely necessary. Although suitable abrasive papers can be found in most tool shops, the polishing agents are stocked only by shops specializing in lapidary equipment, popularly known as 'rock shops', and there is no way of working without them. It is a complete waste of time to try to polish hard stones with toothpaste, whiting, household cleaners, powdered pumice and so forth, although there are one or two easily obtained products which have limited possibilities such as jewellers' rouge, emery and tripoli.

Rock shops are not very common, so the best way to find one is to buy a copy of a lapidary magazine and look at the advertisements. Many of these shops issue catalogues and are willing to sell small quantities by mail order. In case of doubt it is a good idea to explain your position and ask for advice. It is also well worth while subscribing to one of the regular lapidary magazines, and a beginner will be well advised to join a club (the magazines give details of local lapidary clubs), and so benefit from the advice of experienced people.

1 HOW TO POLISH A PEBBLE

Essential materials

The following materials are essential for polishing, and must be bought from a lapidary shop. At least two sheets each of wet and dry silicon carbide abrasive papers are required of grades 100, 300 and 500, or the nearest available. For the fine grade (500), corundum paper can be substituted for silicon carbide. These papers can be bought in good tool shops, but make quite sure that they are waterproof, and that they are not in fact glass papers or emery papers which are not suitable for most lapidary work. Some experienced workers prefer abrasive cloths which are excellent but cost more than paper. For a start two polishing powders will polish most kinds of pebble, a brand of aluminium oxide known as Linde A and cerium oxide. A stick or two of dopwax and some quick setting epoxy resin completes the shopping list.

Linde A is expensive and should be used very sparingly. Although it is only aluminium oxide, the particles are extremely fine, being no more than 0.3 microns in size. Some shops offer an unbranded 0.3 micron pure alumina powder which is cheaper and will do very well. These powders are light in weight and a little goes a long way, so 20 grams ($\frac{2}{3}$ oz) will polish a whole heap of stones. A fault made by many beginners is to assume that if a small amount of polishing powder gives good results then a thicker concentration will give better ones; this is not true and it is wasteful. Linde A used on a leather buff will put a polish on most stones which are not hard, that is, stones which can be scratched with a good penknife. For harder stones like flint, quartz or agate, cerium or tin oxide are best. Cerium oxide is now widely used instead of tin oxide, which has become rather expensive, and it will be useful to buy at least 100 grams (4 oz). It gives good results on a felt rather than a leather buff, but even better ones on a sheet of soft PVC plastic (the kind of thin transparent film sometimes used to put on top of tablecloths).

The hardness of the stone is a key factor of great practical importance, and a complete discussion of hardness appears in chapter 3. Certain combinations of polishing agent and buff or lap have proved to be the best for certain minerals, and these are the ones usually recommended in books. However, the whole process of polishing is wide open for personal experiment and nearly every lapidary has his own special recipe. It frequently happens that a stone which obstinately refuses to polish with one combination will straightaway come up brilliantly with a change of polish or lap.

Dopwax is similar to sealing wax, and it is used for fixing a stone on the end of a short stick so that it can be handled more easily. Dopping is an important part of lapidary work, and the process is fully treated in chapter 7. Although one can polish a pebble without dopping it, there comes a moment in the final polishing when the pebble all too easily slips from one's grip and flies across the room. This can also happen if the dopping has been badly done and the stone comes off the dop, and few things are more frustrating than a pretty stone cracked or chipped just at the moment when the final brilliant polish is beginning to appear—hence the need for dopping a pebble before polishing it.

Checklist of materials

Wet and dry silicon carbide abrasive papers
Linde A
Cerium oxide
Buff (of felt, leather or PVC)
Dopwax
Dopstick
Epoxy resin

Adhesives

There are five different types of glue mentioned in this book. Three of them are used for different processes in lapidary work and the other two for making things in general. For sticking wood there is a very convenient, waterproof, synthetic resin glue which sets quickly. It looks like white cream, can be bought anywhere and only a very thin coating is needed to make a good joint.

For sticking leather or rubber to each other or to wood or stone the best adhesive seems to be one of the contact glues containing neoprene. Two surfaces are each given a coating and allowed to dry, and when they are pressed together the bond is immediate. Care is needed because if the two surfaces are out of alignment no correction is possible.

Two relatively new kinds of glue are useful both for dopping stones and for making apparatus because they will stick stone to metal and also metal to metal strongly enough in many cases to do away with the need for soldering or brazing. Two conditions are necessary for success; first the surfaces to be joined must be a good fit, and secondly they must be free from grease. Cleaning the surfaces with acetone and then not touching them again with the fingers will solve the problem of grease. Filing and rubbing down with abrasive paper will prepare flat surfaces.

One of these adhesives is known as epoxy resin and it comes in two separate tubes, one being a hardener. There are two different kinds, the quick setting and the ordinary ones, and for the lapidary the quick setting

Fig. 1 Materials required for polishing pebbles: frame, leather and PVC laps, polishing powders and silicon carbide papers; it all weighs less than 0.4 kg (1 lb)

one is best because there is always some difficulty in preventing a stone from sliding about before the glue sets. Epoxy resins will stick almost everything except some plastics.

There is an adhesive which has only recently come onto the market which is quite expensive, and has to be used with extreme care. It must be kept out of reach of young children. Sold under a variety of brand names, alpha cyanocrylate glues are usually sold in small plastic tubes containing about 3 grams ($\frac{1}{8}$ oz), which will give between 150 to 200 single drops with care. This glue will not fill up spaces, but it does penetrate cracks, so it is useful for strengthening cracked stones. If two surfaces are perfectly flat and smooth one spot of alpha glue will join them together firmly enough to withstand considerable strain. When a joint needs to be broken, both alpha glue and epoxy resin can be dissolved if immersed for some time in acetone. A quicker way is to heat them to 200°C (392°F), (the temperature needed to roast a chicken), and then they lose their grip, especially if the two objects are twisted rather than pulled apart.

The last glue is one which makes life much easier for lapidaries because abrasive discs can be changed without having to unscrew a nut every time. This glue is a type of rubber cement which remains tacky for a long time; in America it is known as 'peel 'em off' cement, and in Britain 'on/off' cement. The one marketed by the 3M Company is called 'Feathering Disc Adhesive'. This glue does not seem to be stocked by any shops except those dealing in lapidary supplies. It is packaged in spray cans, but tubes or tins, if available, are much easier to handle. This glue is only needed for work on a wheel but experiments to find a substitute using syrup, honey, etc, have been a messy failure.

Not a glue, but sticky nevertheless, is the plastic adhesive tape used for sealing parcels and sold in rolls of different widths. The lapidary will find a roll 2 cm (1 in) wide useful for many jobs.

Making a pebble polisher

This simple device has been designed to be as light and compact as possible so that it can be transported on holidays. It is in two parts, a frame and a polishing pad, and the finished pad should fit snugly inside the frame when not in use.

Materials for the frame

Two pieces of wood 36 x 2 x 1 cm ($14\frac{1}{2}$ x $\frac{3}{4}$ x $\frac{1}{2}$ in).

Two pieces of wood 7.5 x 2 x 1 cm (3 x $\frac{3}{4}$ x $\frac{1}{2}$ in).

One piece of waterproof plastic sheet with a woven backing large enough to cover the frame, 40 × 12 cm (15 × 5 in). (Any remnant will do, such as the piece of imitation leather shown in the illustration.)

Some waterproof glue for fixing the cover and making the frame.

Materials for the polishing pad

One piece of thin wood or hardboard about 5 mm ($\frac{1}{4}$ in) thick, 30 cm (12 in) long, and 6 cm ($2\frac{1}{2}$ in) wide.

One piece of soft padding 27 cm (11 in) long and 6 cm ($2\frac{1}{2}$ in) wide. This can be soft rubber, felt or moquette carpet, etc. Foam plastic tends to collapse under pressure. Two or three strips of draught excluder placed side by side will do perfectly.

One piece of coarse leather with a rough surface 27 cm (11 in) long and 8.5 cm ($3\frac{1}{2}$ in) wide, or wide enough to be taken round the edges of the wood.

One piece of PVC plastic sheet about 2 mm ($\frac{3}{32}$ in) thick, according to what is available. This is useful for polishing stones, and a length of 0.5 m ($\frac{1}{2}$ yd) cut from the roll will come in handy.

One length of strong nylon cord about 2 m (6 ft) long.

Neoprene glue.

Assembling the frame and polishing pad

Place the long strips of wood parallel to each other with the shorter ones inside, all of them standing on their narrow edges, and nail and/or glue them together to form a rectangle 36 cm ($14\frac{1}{2}$in) by 10.5 cm (4 in). Cover this frame tightly with the piece of plastic and fix it all round with glue, staples or drawing pins (thumb tacks) to make a kind of drum.

The polishing pad has 2.5 cm (1 in) of wood uncovered at one end. First glue the padding to the wood; if moquette or draught excluder is used, put it bottom side up. Fit the leather over the padding, rough side up, take it round the edges and glue it on the back of the wood. If only a narrow strip of leather is available, do not stick it in the middle but cover one edge with it, because a covered edge is needed for polishing stones which have an inside curve and cannot be reached with a flat pad.

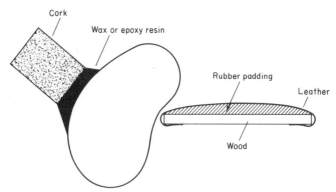

Cork

Wax or epoxy resin

Rubber padding

Leather

Wood

The best kind of leather for this purpose is one with a fairly rough grain; scrap leather from ladies' handbags or boots can be used, even though there may have to be a join somewhere. Where the leather stops short before the end of the wood, cut a small notch on either side of the wood to receive a loop of nylon cord. The leather polishing pad is now complete; it will be used for polishing soft stones with Linde A.

Another pad is needed for cerium oxide and this is made from PVC sheet. A neat arrangement is to make a sheath from the PVC which can be pulled over the leather. Wrap a length of PVC round the leather, not too tightly, and join it up at the back with a length of adhesive tape. Alternatively it can be spot welded together with a hot nail. This sheath will protect the leather pad from contamination when not in use, but the PVC also needs to be protected by a plastic or paper bag. Finally tie a loop in the nylon cord and fix it round the end of the polishing pad.

A very efficient polishing pad for hard stones can easily be made from a plastic bottle with flat sides. Make sure the stopper is airtight by filling up any hole in it, and then tie string round the neck to make a double loop. Wipe off any printed matter with a rag soaked in acetone and remove the label. One side can be covered with leather if preferred. A bottle can be made slightly concave by expelling some of the air, or convex by filling it up with water.

Fig. 2 Polishing a flint pebble on an empty detergent bottle; note the small pulley wheel hooked to a key

Selecting a pebble

The pebble polisher has been made, but before using it something needs to be said about the nature of the pebble. On the assumption that a lapidary, like a language student, is eager for results, the physical properties of various minerals and where they can be found will be considered later on. It is assumed that you have a pebble which looked pretty when it was wet but rather dull when dry, and you have no idea what it is made of. The object of polishing is to give it a wet look for all time, and the first thing to do is to find out how hard the pebble is. As a general rule, hard stones will take a much higher polish than soft ones, but there are exceptions.

Test for hardness by scratching one edge—not the best face—with the point of a good penknife or the corner of a file. If these do not scratch the stone, or only with difficulty, then it can be considered hard. Occasionally a pebble is made of more than one kind of mineral and some parts of it are harder than others.

Another factor which has a bearing on the final polish is the structure of the stone. A pebble of flint or chalcedony which has a smooth, fine surface will take a high polish, although when picked up it may have a rough surface crust which must be ground away. There are other kinds of pebble which are so coarse grained that there is no possibility of polishing them; one might as well try to polish a lump of brick or concrete. Test the pebble for hardness and examine it carefully using a good magnifying glass.

A big advantage in starting with a pebble is that much of the lapidary's work has already been done by water which has rounded the original stone and removed sharp edges. In many cases there is no point in using the coarsest abrasive paper (100 grit) and one can go straight to the medium grade (300 grit). On the other hand some pebbles may have a bump or rough spot which needs to be rubbed down with a piece of flat silicon carbide stone—the kind which is used for sharpening garden tools.

The first attempt at polishing should therefore be made on a smooth-grained pebble with convex surfaces all round and no bumps or hollows, and one that is not too big.

Fig. 3 Collection of hand polished pebbles with a 'wet' look

15

Dopping the pebble

Knowing how to dop stones is an essential part of the lapidary's skill and it takes some practice to master the technique, so the beginner can take a short cut and fix the pebble on the end of an ordinary cork from a wine bottle using quick-setting epoxy resin. When the glue sets, the end of the cork can be trimmed up with a sharp knife.

When one side of the pebble has been sanded smooth and polished, it must be taken off the dop and reversed ready for work on the other half. This is easily done by cutting it away with a knife and scraping off any bits of cork and epoxy resin. Should the stone be soft enough for the polish to be spoilt by scraping, it can be soaked in a small jar of acetone until the glue has dissolved.

Sanding

Everything done so far has been preparatory work; now the serious business of sanding and polishing begins. Sanding is the term used for rubbing a stone smooth with abrasives, whether it be done by hand or on a machine. The technique is to change the original rough surface of a stone, step by step, to a very smooth one and then polish it. Unless the surface has been properly prepared by sanding, no amount of polishing will give results, and the most important step is the final sanding before polishing. For a pebble three different sandings will be enough, on coarse, medium and fine grade silicon carbide paper.

Anybody who is likely to have a constant supply of good pebbles to polish should buy a tumbler instead of doing the work by hand. There are many models from which to choose, but the procedure is the same for all rotary tumblers; a load of stones all of the same hardness is put in a cylindrical drum with loose silicon carbide grit and water, and the drum revolves non-stop day and night. From time to time the grit is changed to a finer grade, and after about three weeks all the stones will be brilliantly polished. However, tumbling stones is rather a dead-end occupation which can be compared to laundering clothes in a washing machine. The results are gratifying, but operating the machine is not very exciting, and one does not become a lapidary by doing it.

Polishing the odd pebble by hand is more amusing and it leads to more advanced lapidary work. Whichever process is used, the sequence is the same; all the scratches made by coarse grit must be removed by a finer one and care must be taken each time that no grit is carried over from the

Diag. 2 Section through a pebble polisher

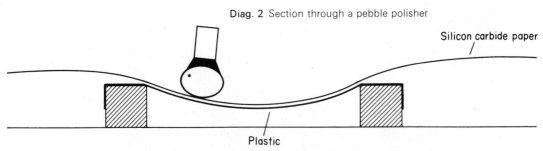

Silicon carbide paper

Plastic

previous stage, because if it is there will be unwanted scratches. The more scratches or pits there are on a finished stone the less light will be reflected and the duller the stone will appear. At the end of each stage the pebble should be dried and carefully inspected under a magnifying glass; if there are any rough patches or obvious scratches it should be returned for more sanding. This really is a case of 'more haste, less speed' because if the work is skimped the only way to put it right is to go back to the beginning and do it over again.

When the pebble is firmly on the dop, take a sheet of 100 grit silicon carbide paper and soak it for a moment in water until it softens, then lay it on top of the frame. There is no point in cutting sheets of paper into strips, it is easier to work with whole sheets. Hold the cork and stone firmly and with plenty of water on both paper and frame begin rubbing up and down the length of the frame with a fair amount of pressure. The plastic will give under pressure so that the best part of the surface of the pebble is in contact

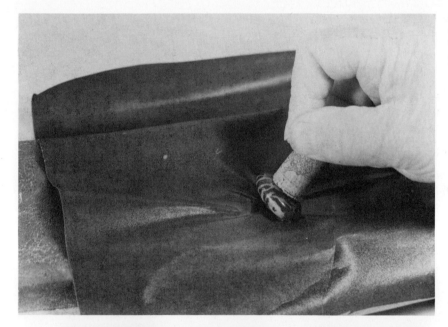

Fig. 4 Sanding a pebble dopped on a cork, using a whole sheet of abrasive paper over the frame

Fig. 5 The plastic gives under pressure and conforms to the outline of the pebble

17

with the paper and the abrasive action produces a well-rounded surface and not one with a series of flat spots which might be the case if the sanding is done on a flat surface. As the pebble is being rubbed up and down it should be rotated and tipped from side to side, so that all exposed parts receive the same treatment.

After a time, dry the stone and examine it carefully, and if the surface appears to be uniform it is time to change to the medium grit. Take away the sheet of 100 grit paper, wash the frame, the pebble and your hands to remove any odd grains of coarse abrasive and repeat the process using 300 paper. The strict drill of washing away all traces of abrasive when making a change is an absolutely necessary part of all lapidary work no matter what equipment is in use. Contamination must always be avoided, so care must be taken in the storage of grits and abrasive papers so that they do not get mixed up. Obviously a polishing pad contaminated with particles of coarse grit is worse than useless.

When a satisfactory surface has been obtained with 300 grit paper the final sanding is done with 500, and at this stage the stone may already begin to take on a slight lustre and any pattern in it will show up more clearly than before. Make absolutely certain that there are no unwanted scratches, because they will still be there when the stone is polished, and this is the time to go back and sand them out.

There is a natural tendency to do more work on the face of the pebble and not enough on the sides; this occurs not only in pebble polishing but in making cabochons too, so this is the time to correct a bad habit. If there is any doubt about the finish of the stone at this stage, go on sanding for a few more minutes; it will pay.

Polishing

If the sanding has been well done the actual polishing takes very little time, but no amount of polishing will compensate for incomplete sanding. If, during polishing, it is obvious that there are going to be dull spots due to scratches, the only thing to do is to return to the frame and do some more sanding. There is no satisfaction to be had from a polished stone marred by blemishes which are a permanent witness to sloppy workmanship. This is true for all lapidary work on any kind of equipment, whether the stone be a simple pebble, a cabochon or a faceted gem. The lapidary must never be content with second best, the goal must always be perfection.

The sanding process is standard for all kinds of materials but there is considerable variation in polishing methods depending on the nature of the mineral in hand. Most soft stones can be polished on a leather lap using a small quantity of Linde A powder, and a good way to avoid waste is to put a layer of the powder in a small, transluscent plastic oil can, and then add water in the proportion of ten to one. The powder soon sinks to the bottom and if there is too much water some of it can be poured off. Tap water may be perfectly safe for drinking but it is not always good for stone polishing because it may contain minute particles of sand or lime which will spoil a polish. Distilled water is better, and so is water from the ice which forms in a refrigerator as neither kind will contain unwanted abrasives. If some of this water is kept in a plastic squeeze bottle, it can be used for moistening laps when they dry out but do not need more polishing powder.

Shake the oil can well until the powder is in suspension and then pour some on the polishing lap, spreading it out with a finger tip until it sinks into the leather. The pebble is now rubbed vigorously up and down until a polish is obtained. If the pebble is a hard one then the PVC sheath is drawn over the leather and this lap is charged with cerium oxide in the same way. The cerium oxide can also be kept in an oil can or a glass jar, covered with water as before; it can be transferred from the jar with a small water colour paint brush kept only for that purpose and always kept free from contamination.

Polishing laps dry out very quickly in a warm room and if a stone is rubbed hard on dry polishing powder it will be scratched and not polished. For this reason the condition of the lap, especially at the edges must be checked frequently with a finger tip and more liquid added or water sprayed on. In any case very little powder is needed in polishing and it is better to be mean rather than over generous. From time to time old polish should be washed off laps and a fresh coating put on, the washing being done with pure water.

If, after hard rubbing up and down on the lap, there is no significant result two things can be done, the first being to change from one lap to the other, not forgetting to clean the pebble. If there is still no polish, it may be that the speed is too low and that not enough frictional heat is being generated. There is a definite limit to the speed at which a stone can be moved across a lap by hand and this speed is very much slower than that obtained with a revolving wheel.

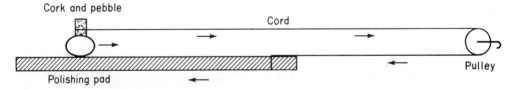

Diag. 3 Attaching nylon cord to the cork and polishing pad

This is where the nylon cord is brought into play; it is attached to the lap by making a slip knot and pulling the loop tight inside the two notches. A loop is also made in the other end and pulled tight round the cork on which the pebble is dopped. If the lap is held in one hand and the cord passed round some convenient smooth fixture such as a door knob, and the pebble held in the other hand, it will be found that when the pebble is moved forwards the lap moves backwards and vice versa. The effect of this is to double the speed of the stone in relation to the lap and this will usually do the trick and bring up a polish. The movement is a little awkward to do at first, but it comes right with practice. There is one inconvenience in that the nylon cord soon wears out where it goes round the door knob and it is therefore much better to use a small pulley wheel.

Fig. 6 Doubling the relative
speed with a length of cord
looped round a door knob

This pebble polisher is so small and easy to use that one can polish beach
pebbles in a hotel bedroom, and as quite the best time to hunt for attractive
pebbles is when they are wet, there is no need to be bored on a rainy day by
the seaside.

Awkward shaped pebbles

Nature does not produce every pretty pebble in just the right shape for
polishing with convex surfaces all round, some may have hollows or
unwelcome bumps which have to be taken into account. There are two
solutions to this problem, one being to polish only that part of the pebble
which can be done easily leaving the rest in its natural state. This makes an
interesting contrast but it is not to everyone's taste. The other solution is to
grind away part of the pebble to remove a bump or convert a hollow into a
saddle which can be polished on the edge of the lap. If there is not much
material to be removed it can be done by hand with a flat piece of silicon
carbide grindstone with a fairly coarse grain. Beware of altering the
original shape of a pebble too much; there is a charm about a natural shape
which is soon lost when the outline is modified artificially.

When the polishing lap was made the leather was taken round the edges
for the express purpose of being able to polish saddle-shaped hollows, but
of course it is impossible to polish the bottom of a dish-shaped depression
with such a lap. The sanding frame was made to cope with convex
surfaces, and it is not used for concave ones. Instead, the abrasive papers
are laid over something soft and cylindrical in shape; a tightly rolled
newpaper or magazine will do. After a time there will be no difficulty in
deciding which shaped pebbles can be polished all over and which will
have to receive alternative treatment.

At this point a pebble has now been polished entirely by hand for the first
time, and it is more than probable that it has some defects; there may be
places round the edge where the polish has been skimped or perhaps an
unfortunate scratch has been left. The perfectionist will go back to the
beginning and do the work over again but one has to be a hero to sand
away a polish which has been so painstakingly achieved, so keep the first
pebble and resolve to do better next time. This is one way of polishing a
pebble but it is not the most efficient nor the way to bring best results, it is
the simplest way to begin lapidary work.

Aftercare

When all is done and the pebble has been removed from the dop and thoroughly cleaned with a few drops of detergent in water, there may be a temptation to go back and give just a little extra rub on the polishing lap. This should be resisted, because the chances are that, unless the stone is dopped once more, it will slip from one's grip and be spoilt. It is better to cheat a little and give the stone a rub with silicon impregnated paper, the kind used for cleaning spectacles or the coarser kind offered by hotels for cleaning shoes.

It is a curious fact that nine times out of ten the first thing a man does when shown a polished pebble is to start rubbing it on his sleeve or trouser leg to improve the shine. This seems to be an automatic reflex, but it must be stopped immediately because the minute specks of household dust which settle on everything, including trousers, are as hard as most stones and coarser than the particles of polishing powder which were used. The result is that trouser rubbing spoils a polish rather than improves it. It is on account of dust that polishing laps must be wrapped up when not in use. Sanding papers too should be stored in such a way that grains from the coarser grades do not contaminate other sheets. A convenient arrangement is to keep sheets between the pages of an old magazine, fine grade at the top and coarse at the bottom.

When a collection of polished pebbles has been built up they can be displayed on a dish, but they should not be heaped on top of each other. A useful way of storing them is in drawer lined with a sheet of polystyrene (styrofoam) which can be hollowed out to fit each individual stone.

Fig. 7 A dish of assorted, polished pebbles

2 WORKING WITH PEBBLES

Mineralogy and palaeontology

What is a pebble? 'A small stone, less than a boulder, worn and rounded by the action of water' says the dictionary. Pebbles are fascinating objects; quite a number of books have been written about them and the London Museum of Natural History staged an exhibition entirely devoted to pebbles. At some time or another almost everybody picks up a pebble to take a closer look, and this gesture has led more than one person to make a serious study of mineralogy. It is directly responsible for the production of this book.

There are pebbles which glitter in the sun and defy all attempts at polishing them; others are so smooth and symmetrical that without any further treatment they can be pocketed as 'worry stones' to be caressed between finger and thumb during moments of stress. Some types of rock are ground into flat disc-shaped pebbles, whereas others become more egg-shaped, and there are those which just crumble into sand.

The dilettante pebble collector may well start meditating on the nature of pebbles, where they come from, what they are made of, why on some beaches they are all alike and on others there is great variety, or why sometimes pebbles are not on beaches but high up in hills and mountains far removed from sea or lakes. Inevitably if he has any sense of curiosity at all the pebbler will be drawn to find out more about them and consult a book on elementary geology. This will explain that pebbles come from three main types of rock—sedimentary, igneous and metamorphic—and that in addition to having been formed in streams or by the sea they may

Fig. 8 Three 'worry stones' shaped by nature and polished by hand

22

Fig. 9 Curious pebbles of calcareous rock honeycombed by some form of marine life

Fig. 10 A slice of sedimentary rock (stromatolite) and three pebbles formed from it

have fallen out of boulder clay or have been carried for hundreds of miles by glaciers millions of years ago. One of the great delights of becoming a lapidary is to discover so much of interest in the world of stones. Shakespeare was right when he wrote in *As You Like It* '. . . books in the running brook, sermons in stones and good in everything'.

Knowing what type of rock the pebble came from is a step towards knowing what it is made of and how it will respond to grinding and polishing, in other words it is an introduction to mineralogy. A pretty, speckled, pink and black pebble may be identified as coming from cliffs of red granite and according to the dictionary granite is 'a granular, crystalline rock consisting essentially of quartz, orthoclase-feldspar and mica'. Here is the technical vocabulary of the specialist, and even if a layman thinks he knows how to recognize quartz or mica he may well be stumped by 'orthoclase-feldspar' and yet it is precisely this substance which is responsible for the pretty pink colour which caught his eye in the first place.

Thus some knowledge of mineralogy, however imperfect, is essential for any serious lapidary; but the subject is so fascinating that it can easily develop into a major interest. The definition of granite includes the word 'crystalline' which introduces a division of mineralogy concerned with

Fig. 11 Pebbles with different kinds of inclusions

Fig. 12 A puzzle pebble: the loose piece inside is too big to pass through the hole

Fig. 13 Pebbles containing fossils

24

crystal systems and this is yet another profound field for research. Obviously there are limits to the pursuit of knowledge, nevertheless anyone who aspires to faceting stones will also have to learn something about cleavage planes, double refraction, critical angles, optical axes and other aspects of crystallography which have important practical significance for a faceter. Likewise, in cutting cabochons from material which produces cat's-eye or star effects the lapidary must know something about the optical peculiarities which produce these phenomena and what causes them, otherwise he will not be able to cut the stone for maximum effect.

The search for interesting pebbles or other minerals is almost certain to uncover fossils. For example many of the flint pebbles on the south coast of England or the north coast of France contain fragments of fossilized marine animals which died millions of years ago. These fossil remains produce interesting patterns when the pebble is polished. The pebble collector will have to be very strong minded not to give way to the temptation of picking up fossils and so entering yet another absorbing branch of knowledge— palaeontology. It is not suggested that people who occasionally would like to polish a pebble must necessarily embark on an advanced course in natural sciences, but there is a real chance, particularly for young people, that they may discover new interests which will endure for a lifetime.

The average household will not be equipped with standard reference books, so further knowledge must be sought in public libraries and museums and in buying suitable books. There are museums with well displayed and well labelled mineral specimens, but unfortunately this section is often neglected in small, local museums and not brought up to date. The book market is much better, there are first class books available with coloured plates, dealing with rocks, minerals, gems and fossils, all at reasonable prices. Once an interest in stones has been aroused, a good source of information is the Encyclopaedia Britannica, published in two distinct versions which are normally to be found side by side in any good library. One version is for quick reference and the other for more detailed information. Good headings to look up are 'gemstones', 'siliceous minerals', 'feldspars' and 'crystals'.

The simple act of stooping to pick up a pebble opens the gates to a fantastic world where recent research on quartz crystals found in a cave high in the Swiss Alps proves that 16 million years were needed for them to complete their growth; sermons in stones are a reality.

Pebble mosaics

The Italians are very skilful at making decorative pavements out of pebble mosaics and the same technique in miniature will produce mosaic pictures from unpolished pebbles. The first thing to do is to build up a collection of small flat pebbles in various different colours, black, white, yellow, grey etc. They should be about the size of finger or thumb nails, and flat rather than rounded because they will stand on edge. Suitable subjects for mosaic pictures are birds and fishes which can be done in two or three

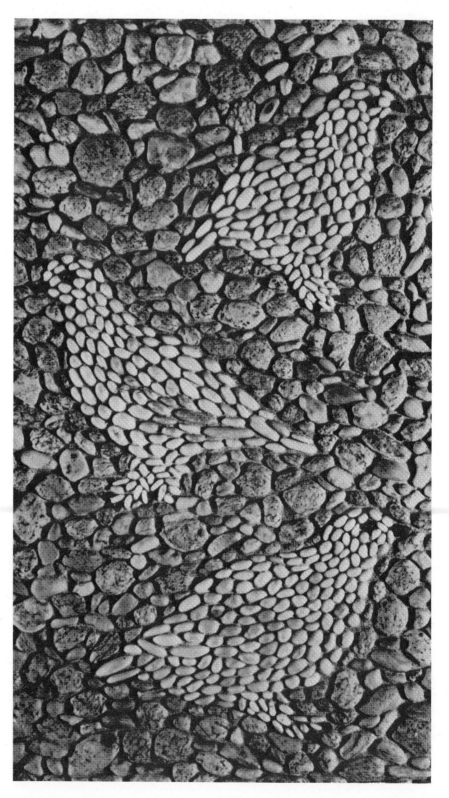

Fig. 14 Pebble mosaic picture by Lors Olsommer, 'Snow partridges', 45 x 68 cm (18 x 27 in)

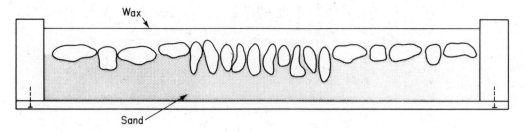

Diag. 4 Making a pebble mosaic

colours surrounded by a uniform background carried out in somewhat larger pebbles.

The technique is simple. First the design is drawn on paper full size then a wooden frame is made from wood about 2.5 cm (1 in) thick and 7.5 cm (3 in) wide to go round it. Fix a plywood or hardboard bottom to the frame with adhesive tape or one or two short nails so that it can be removed easily. Half fill the box so formed with fine sand and tamp down the surface to a uniform level. The design is next built up from rows of pebbles set side by side on edge, each one pressed into the sand. The sand will later be replaced by concrete, and the pebbles must be pushed in far enough to be gripped by the concrete when the job is finished.

The best effects are obtained with very thin pebbles (like plastic game counters) but advantage can be taken of thickness to suggest plumage or fish scales. Occasionally a stone needs to be broken to produce a fragment for a bird's beak or leg, otherwise the pebbles should be untouched.

When the central design is finished the surrounding background is put in with a contrasting colour. The surface is checked with a straight edge to make sure it is level and then hot, melted paraffin wax (candlegrease) is poured all over it up to the top of the frame. When everything is quite cold and there is not danger of the stones working loose, turn the box upside down, remove the bottom and wash away all the sand. Mix up some runny concrete with one part cement to three parts of builders' sand, and pour it into the frame, then shake and tap the frame to release any air bubbles. A layer of fine wire netting can be put in for greater strength, but in any case there must be loops of wire so that the picture can be hung. Allow several days for the concrete to set hard before removing the frame and getting rid of the wax with a knife and hot water. The lapidary will want to put some kind of a polish to bring up the colour of the stones. This can be done with loose grits and polishing pads. (The use of loose grit is explained in chapter 4.)

These mosaic pictures make attractive and unusual displays, but they are heavy and need good anchorage on the wall.

3 HARDNESS OF STONES

Hardness and toughness

The hardness of a stone is of great importance to the lapidary because it determines his method of working, but the average person has misconceived ideas about hardness. Somebody is said to be 'as hard as nails' or 'a man of steel', but when it comes to sharpening a steel tool it is ground away on a piece of stone. Steel tools are quite useless for cutting hard gemstones and there is not one which will make any impression on a piece of jade, let alone diamond. Steel is strong and tough, but it will not rate very high on any scale of hardness.

The metal saws and drills used for cutting gemstones are impregnated with tiny particles of diamond and it is the diamond which does the cutting, not the metal. Diamond-impregnated tools are products of recent technology, and as they have now come within reach of amateur craftsmen, lapidary work is no longer confined to a few professionals.

In 1812 a German mineralogist, Friedrich Mohs, devised a scale of hardness from 1 to 10 using a series of different minerals each one of which would scratch the one below it on the scale but not the one above. Mohs' scale is still used today, because hardness is one of the first tests in determining the nature of an unknown mineral. It is important to understand that the numbers on the scale do not represent a regular graduation in the way a ruler does, with the result that a mineral rated at 8 is not twice as hard as one rated at 4, while a diamond, rated at 10, is hundreds of times harder than quartz, which has a score of 7. Today scientists have devised more sophisticated means for testing hardness and measuring it in absolute rather than relative units, but Mohs' scale is quite sufficient for the amateur lapidary.

Mohs' Scale

1	Talc	6	Orthoclase
2	Gypsum	7	Quartz
3	Calcite	8	Topaz
4	Fluorite	9	Corundum
5	Apatite	10	Diamond

Fig. 15 Two different forms of gypsum, alabaster and transparent sheets

Fig. 16 Crystals of calcite in a limestone geode

Fig. 17 Three different forms of fluorite, one being Blue John

Fig. 18 Examples of fine carving in jade (Chinese)

Many of these names are not in common use, so further information is given in chapter 13. A few experiments will soon demonstrate how the scale works in practice. Any mineral which is rated at 3 or less can be scratched with a finger nail; one of these is alabaster which is a type of gypsum. Minerals which can be scratched by a copper coin but not a finger nail are rated at 3 or 4 on Mohs' scale. The next handy scratching implement is a penknife, and a good blade will be about $5\frac{1}{2}$ on the scale. Ordinary glass is much the same hardness and is not easily scratched by a knife. This is a useful dividing line in selecting stones which can be used for jewellery, because stones which can be scatched by a knife are not suitable for rings and they are better mounted as pendants where they are less likely to be damaged in wear. Malachite is a good example of a soft stone ($3\frac{1}{2}$–4) used in jewellery, but it needs a mounting which will protect it from being scratched and so losing its polish.

If you try to scratch quartz, chalcedony or flint with a knife it is the point of the blade which is worn away while the stone remains untouched, although a good steel file with a hardness of 6 to 7 may make some impression. The sharp edge of a piece of flint or quartz will easily cut a groove in a bottle, so a useful thing for testing minerals in the field is a small piece of glass; anything which scratches it will be at least 6 on Mohs' scale. This degree of hardness represents a good dividing line between the lapidary and a mason or a sculptor, both of whom use metal tools for shaping stone. If marble were really hard there would be far fewer statues made out of it.

Minerals of hardness 7 or more cannot be shaped with metal, they have to be ground with abrasives or cut with diamond-impregnated tools. Until recent times the only abrasives used were those found in nature, for example crushed garnets with a hardness of 6 to $7\frac{1}{2}$.

Fig. 19 Stone Age axe head with a drilled hole

Relics from early civilizations in parts of the world as far apart as China and Central America prove that man had mastered the art of carving minerals as hard and as tough as jade ($6\frac{1}{2}$–7) using natural abrasives. Anyone who has tried working jade with modern machines and abrasives cannot fail to be awed by the skill and patience with which artists of long ago made the beautiful objects which have survived and which are to be seen in the world's museums. It is a valuable experience to have a long look at these masterpieces whenever the opportunity occurs.

Basically the technique was to wear away the stone with abrasives held in place by comparatively soft material such as bamboo cane or reeds. There are polished Stone Age axe heads to be seen in museums, beautifully ground from hard stone, and some have a neat round hole drilled from side to side for the shaft to fit in. These holes were made with the equivalent of a modern core drill because in some cases the core or plug removed from the axe head has been found. Presumably the drilling was done with a hollow reed rotated by a bow and the end covered with wet silica sand, but it must have been a very slow process. One wonders whether the primitive hunter had the patience to do this, or whether he left the womenfolk to do it while he went hunting.

Fig. 20a Pre-historic North American Indian arrow heads carved from flint and obsidian (courtesy Werner Forman Archive)

Fig. 20b Chinese spear head (c 700 BC) and arrow head made from jade (c 200 BC)

32

Cleavage

Stones, like all other matter, are composed of atoms which determine their physical characteristics of resistance to hammering or scratching. Resistance to scratching can be measured on any surface of a stone, and it can be demonstrated that in some cases one surface or the point of a crystal is harder than another, or even that there can be a difference in hardness according to the direction of the scratch. Herein lies the answer to a puzzling question; if diamond is the hardest substance on this earth, how is it possible to cut a faceted diamond? The answer lies in the atomic structure of the diamond crystal which is responsible for weaknesses called cleavage planes.

Although it is hard, a diamond is brittle, and will split along these planes when dealt a sharp blow in the right place. Many minerals have cleavage planes, for example fluorite will split in four different directions, but quartz does not have any. However many times a diamond splits and becomes smaller, the points of the crystals are harder than the faces. The professional faceter takes synthetic diamonds which have been crushed to a fine powder, and uses this to facet a gem, because when he puts the powder on a revolving metal lap and presses the diamond down on it, there will always be some points sticking up which will be harder than the face of the diamond, and so it will slowly be ground as he wants it.

When two different minerals have the same hardness, one may still be much tougher to work than the other, or it may be more brittle and liable to crack. The lapidary soon finds this out when he starts work on a stone, and the skilled worker takes advantage of any peculiarities. On account of its exceptional toughness, jade in the hands of Chinese craftsmen is carved into intricate and wonderful patterns which would be impossible in a more brittle material.

Strike a rock repeatedly with a hammer and in the end the rock will split, even though it be harder than the hammer. Different rocks split in different ways depending on their atomic structure, some will easily break along their cleavage planes, but those without any will divide into irregular pieces or flake off with the typical conchoidal fractures of flint or obsidian. Primitive man took advantage of this flaking to make knives and arrowheads out of flint.

Hardness, toughness, cleavage, fracture from pressure or heat are all factors the lapidary cannot afford to neglect. You will find directions for dealing with well-known minerals in all lapidary books, and this is the record of past experience. By taking advantage of what is known, and at the same time recording in a notebook one's own personal findings, it is possible to build up a fund of useful knowledge. It is folly to spend a long time working on a stone and then to have it crack or discolour at the polishing stage because you neglected to find out whether it is heat sensitive or not.

4 FLAT LAPPING

When a pebble is polished, very little is done to alter its natural shape and so all surfaces remain curved. The next step in learning the lapidary's craft is to polish a flat surface, which is a more difficult thing to do. It is the beginning of faceting because all a faceter does is to grind a series of flat surfaces in precise positions and then polish them. One can begin flat lapping with rough pieces of broken rock which have at least one face more or less flat, or one can buy ready-sawn slices from a rock shop. A chunk of mineral with just one face polished makes a most attractive display specimen showing the contrast between a natural surface and man's artifice. Flat slices with a hole drilled through them can make very pretty pendants. Polishing flat surfaces is a slow business which can easily become tedious, so it is best to start with something small; a slice the size of a big postage stamp would not be too big.

Materials required

Flat lapping is done with loose silicon carbide grits on sheets of flat glass or steel. Three grades of grit are needed from a lapidary supplier, one bag each of numbers 100, 300 and 500 or the nearest available. Grits are normally packaged in 0.5 k (1 lb) bags, but the coarse one (100) will be used up faster than the others. At the same time buy a small quantity, 250 grams ($\frac{1}{2}$ lb), of aluminium oxide powder of the grade used for pre-polishing in tumblers. Polishing powders, Linde A and cerium oxide, are required as used for polishing pebbles.

From a glazier, obtain four or five sheets of plate glass. Salvage glass is all that is needed, and you can cut it to size yourself. Failing that, thick window glass can be used, but it breaks more easily. The sizes can vary, but for good working each piece should be not much smaller than a page of this book or a dinner plate. It is an advantage for all the pieces to be of the same thickness. One can flat lap on one piece of glass, but this means that for each change of grit all the grit has to be washed off and this is a waste of grit and of time.

Storing five sheets of glass each covered with a different grit or powder is rather a problem, and keeping them in plastic bags is not the best solution because the grit soon finds its way to the underside of the glass as well as on top and this makes a mess. More troublesome but well worth

Fig. 21 A slice of malachite lapped and polished by hand makes a decorative pendant

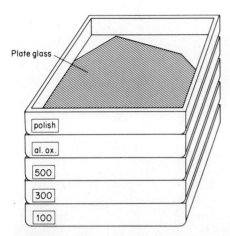

Plate glass

polish
al. ox.
500
300
100

Diag. 5 Stack of trays for flat lapping

Fig. 22 Sheets of salvage glass need not entirely cover the base of a tray for flat lapping

while is to find a shallow tray for each sheet and store them one above the other in a carton with the coarse grade at the bottom and the polishing powder on top, to avoid contamination. Trays can be made of hardboard with a strip of wood all round, but plastic seed trays with the edges cut down are very neat and waterproof. When you buy seed trays, buy one or two thin canes about 60 cm (2 ft) long as well. Cut pieces of plate glass to fit inside these seed trays, but there is no need for them to cover the bottom completely. Label each tray clearly with the size of grit or polishing powder for which it is to be used.

Warning concerning sink blockage

When using loose grits, it is necessary constantly to wash hands, stones and sometimes pieces of glass. Silicon carbide grit is heavy and if it is poured down the sink it will settle in bends in the pipe and eventually build up a solid deposit which hardens like cement, and the plumber's bill will be a big one. Keep a bowl for washing and after a time the grit will settle and most of the water can be poured off. The residue can be thrown on the garden, or in the case of apartment dwellers, filtered through a large flower pot about one third full of fine earth. Young lapidaries who ignore this warning will be extremely unpopular.

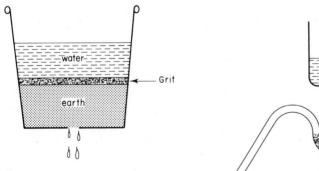

water

Grit

earth

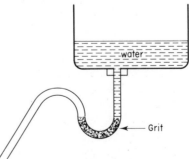

water

Grit

Diag. 6 A flower pot filter should be used before pouring water down the sink, to prevent build up of grit in the S bend

Fig. 23 Flat lapping on glass
with a scrubbing movement

Method of flat lapping

If the pieces are big enough to take hold of there is no need to dop them for flat lapping; small pieces can be dopped on a flat-headed bolt or screw. If the glass is not in trays, put a sheet on several thicknesses of newspaper which can be thrown away afterwards, because lapping with loose grit is a messy business. Put a teaspoonful of 100 grit in the middle of the glass and add water to make a paste. The amount of water needed soon becomes apparent as the grit swims about if there is too much and clogs together if not enough.

Hold the surface of the stone parallel to the glass with the most prominent part in contact and move it about with a circular motion like scrubbing a floor. Continue rubbing over all the surface of the glass and changing the direction of rotation from time to time. Obviously if the grit wears away stone it will wear away the glass too and eventually there will be a depression in the glass sheet; this is why the rubbing is spread out over the surface.

With coarse grit even hard minerals soon begin to wear down and present a flat face, and the best results seem to come if only moderate pressure is used and small quantities of fresh grit added frequently as the grains break down. Broken down grains are finer and they still continue to cut but the action is less pronounced. The stone which is ground away mixes with the grit and forms a slurry which thickens until the cutting action is slowed up, so after a time wash all the grit from the glass and start afresh. The surface of the glass can be checked with a straight edge and when it is too uneven it must be changed too, otherwise it will be impossible to grind a flat face on the stone.

Continue lapping on coarse grit until a uniform flat surface has been ground, then wash the stone, dry it and examine it carefully. Irregularities are seen more easily if the stone is dry, and the stone should have the appearance of ground glass, that is, covered all over with minute holes. Subsequent lapping on medium and fine grit reduces the size of these tiny holes until the surface is smooth enough to polish.

Stone and hands are washed free from all traces of coarse grit before taking a second sheet of glass and repeating the process with 300 grit. This washing drill has to be gone through every time a change is made from one abrasive to a finer one because if some grains are carried over the scratches they make will stand out. From this point on it will be taken for granted that when the lapidary grinds, sands and polishes a stone, by whatever method, the necessary precautions will be taken to avoid contamination.

After sanding with 300 grit the stone is lapped with 500 grit followed by aluminium oxide, and there is a very good reason for switching to a different abrasive. For a long time I was disappointed with the results obtained by flat lapping and always failed to raise a really glossy finish until coming across a fact which is not mentioned in most instructions for flat lapping. The cause of failure is that no matter how fine a grade of silicon carbide is used for the final lapping, the surface is still covered with thousands of tiny holes because the cutting action of loose grits is not the same as the action when they are fixed to paper or cloth.

Silicon carbide grit digs holes   Aluminium oxide creates a smooth surface

Diag. 7 Action of loose grit

Silicon carbide, on account of its atomic structure, breaks into small pieces with sharp points which, under pressure between the lap and the stone, dig holes in the stone. The grains break into smaller pieces but these too have sharp points and the hole digging continues although the holes are smaller. By switching to aluminium oxide after 500 silicon carbide this action is halted because the grains of aluminium oxide are rounded and not pointed, and so a much smoother surface can be prepared ready for polishing.

According to the hardness of the stone use Linde A or cerium oxide, the former on leather glued to a flat board, and the latter on a sheet of PVC plastic laid on top of glass. Take care that the cerium oxide does not dry out round the edges because a stone rubbed on the dry powder will be scratched instead of polished.

In the later stages of sanding, and especially when polishing, there is a danger that minute chips will break away from any sharp edges the stone may have and cause serious scratching. The way to prevent this is to grind a slight bevel all round the edge with a piece of grindstone or abrasive paper, and this may need doing several times.

Diag. 8 Chamfering a sharp
edge to prevent chips from
breaking off the stone

Before polishing, check the lap with a finger tip and remove any particles which are apparent. A polish can be considered satisfactory when the dry stone is held underneath an electric light bulb and one can read the voltage and maker's name in its reflection.

There is an alternative to the PVC lap which gives good results for the quartz group, and that is an old LP gramophone record. The polishing powder sinks into the grooves and has to be kept damp. When polishing, a fair amount of pressure is needed and it may be easier to rub the stone backwards and forwards rather than in the circular motion used for sanding. If a soft stone fails to respond to a leather lap try using wood; most things will polish on a soft wood lap such as a piece of plywood, but there are no hard and fast rules about polishing.

There is nothing difficult about flat lapping but it is not a very exciting activity and should not be carried on for too long at a time. If there is sufficient work to justify the expense, the lapidary should buy a vibrating lap which does the job with very little supervision. However, as a perfectly flat surface cannot be produced on a grinding wheel, it is a good plan to have a flat lap within easy reach even when using a machine. A quick rub on coarse grit will make sure that the base of a cabochon is quite flat; it does not need to be polished.

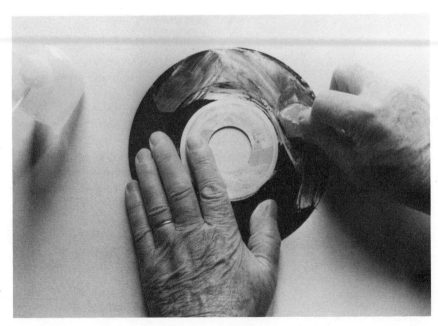

Fig. 24 Splendid for noise
abatement: polishing quartz on
a pop record

38

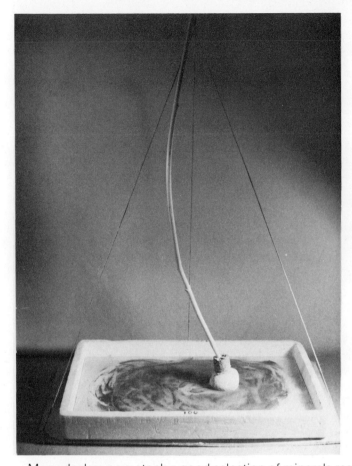

Fig. 25 A simple way of applying pressure to a stone when flat lapping

Many dealers now stock a good selection of minerals ready sliced, and when these are polished they make splendid pieces for a collection, or they can be mounted as pendants. Hand lapping large slices is hard work but some of the effort can be made easier by resurrecting a technique formerly used when sheet glass was polished by hand. Pressure was applied to the work from a long pole wedged between the ceiling and the polishing table.

To make a similar arrangement find a piece of hardboard a little bigger than the trays containing the glass laps, and drill three holes in it. Tie pieces of string in each hole and bring them together at a central point about 60 cm (2 ft) above the glass. Bind them with adhesive tape round the edge of a plastic cap from a ball point pen, or something which will serve the same purpose. A piece of thin cane or a wand of hazel or ash about 6 mm ($\frac{1}{4}$ in) at the thick end is inserted in the cap and half a cork fixed on the bottom end. Pressure on the stone depends on the length of the cane, and it can be varied by packing up the lap on layers of newspaper. A spot of 'on/off cement' on the end of the cork keeps it from slipping off the stone. If the adjustment is right a stone can be moved all over the lap without one having to bear down on it all the time. Although this gadget is useful for big pieces which need a lot of grinding, it is not worth while rigging it up for small pieces.

Fig. 26 Excellent, inexpensive raw material for random faceting: quartz containing needles of rutile and tourmaline

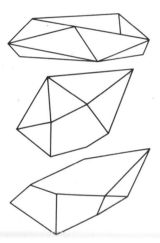

Diag. 9 Random faceted stones

Random facets

Flat lapping can be used to make windows in transparent material. A transparent quartz pebble with a frosted surface becomes much more interesting if a small flat surface is ground and polished in one edge thus making a window to the inside.

There are two kinds of quartz easily bought in small chunks for very little money, one having golden needles of rutile included and the other needles of black tourmaline. These chunks usually have at least one side which can soon be ground flat, and when this is lapped and polished so that the inclusions can be clearly seen the result is very pleasing. Sometimes the opposite side can be polished too and this leads on to random faceting. The entire stone is covered with polished facets with no attempt at symmetry, their position depending entirely on how the natural breaks lie. Any attempt to make a more or less regular shape will not be a success because it will look like badly done conventional faceting. Random faceted stones have a charm of their own, the more so because they are not commonly found in the jewellery trade.

Fig. 27 Random faceted stone of quartz with tourmaline

Although true, large facets can be made when holding the stone in the fingers, it is extremely difficult to produce small ones without some kind of guide.

To make a primitive faceting device take two pieces of hardwood dowelling 1 cm ($\frac{3}{8}$ in) in diameter and 19 cm ($7\frac{1}{2}$ in) long. Cut a small panel 18 x 7 cm (7 x 3 in) from chipboard 1 cm ($\frac{3}{8}$ in) thick. (Chipboard is a tough 'wooden' board made from compressed chips of raw wood.) Glue one of the pieces of dowelling along the short edge of the chipboard with equal projection on either side. Draw a line down the middle of the chipboard, and on it at intervals of 2.5 cm (1 in) bore holes a little smaller than the diameter of the dowelling, then ream them with the handle of a file so that they are slightly conical inside.

Put a long, gradual taper on one end of the other piece of dowelling, which becomes a dopstick. If this taper nearly corresponds to the cone-shaped holes, the dopstick can be pushed firmly into one of them and it will

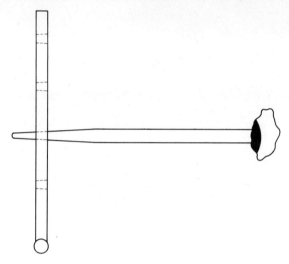

Diag. 10 Jig for random faceting

not fall out or wobble about. The stone to be lapped can be dopped directly on the end of the stick with wax, or else fixed to a metal screw put in the end. With this arrangement the direction of a small facet can be controlled in two ways, first by rotating the dopstick and secondly by choosing different holes and by raising and lowering the height of the base.

The base, which is the horizontal piece of dowelling, rests on a flat board which must always be exactly parallel to the glass lap. A breadboard propped up on a book makes an effective platform. If the device is found to be too light, add extra weight by taping a slice of rock to the bottom, experience will soon show what is needed. This elementary faceting equipment will enable you to put true small facets anywhere on the stone, but it will have to be taken off the dop and reversed at some stage.

The hand faceting unit described in a later chapter is a more refined version of this one, so a little random faceting is an excellent preparation for more complicated work later on.

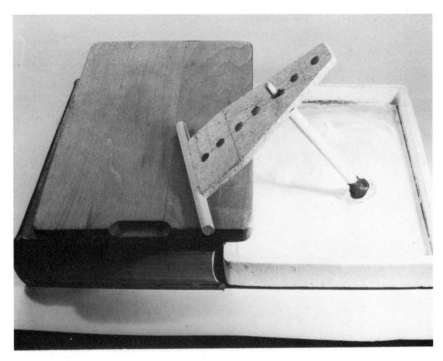

Cutting glass

Four or five sheets of plate glass are needed for flat lapping and it is often possible to pick up salvage plate glass for nothing. Glaziers smash broken shop windows into small pieces and throw them away, and although they may give them to you as they are, they will naturally expect to be well paid for their skill if you ask them to cut the pieces to size. Cutting plate glass is a skilled craft but anyone can make an attempt at it when the final result does not have to be neat or accurate. A diamond glass cutter is not required; a cutter with small steel wheels will do very well.

Lay the sheet of glass on two or three thicknesses of newspaper on a perfectly flat table, making sure there are no bits underneath it. Thoroughly clean the top where the cut is to be made. Find a solid straight-edge (a school ruler is not thick enough), and enlist the help of another person to hold it in place, because if it is not held in place the cut will go wrong.

Make a small scratch with the wheel at the edge of the glass where the line is to come and then put the straight-edge tight up against the cutter. Press down firmly and make one bold sweep from edge to edge without a stop. Do not saw backwards and forwards, the cut should be made with one stroke. Put the glass so that the wanted part lies flat on the table but the cut is on the overhanging piece parallel with the edge of the table and about 5 cm (2 in) away from it.

With the end of a big file, or the sharp edge of a hammer, give a sharp rap on the underside of the glass exactly below the cut and in the middle of the sheet. The tendency is not to hit hard enough, so a few more taps may be

Fig. 29 If a sheet of plate glass is given a sharp tap directly underneath a cut, it will crack as shown here

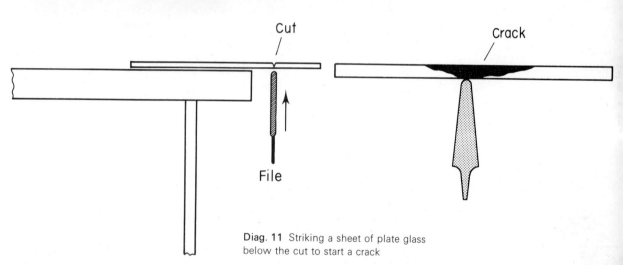

Cut

Crack

File

Diag. 11 Striking a sheet of plate glass below the cut to start a crack

needed before a crack is seen to appear running along the cut. Tapping more gently, first to one side then to the other, lead the crack to the edges and the glass will fall apart.

Should the crack leave the line of the cut and run into the glass you will have to make a fresh start if it is in the piece you want. If it runs into the off-cut then a new crack can be started, but there will probably be a pointed piece left where the two cracks meet. This can be nibbled away with pincers. Rub all edges smooth with a file.

5 PURPOSE AND ORGANIZATION

With a pebble polisher, a set of glass laps, bags of loose grit and a jig for random faceting, a new hobby begins to grow and take up more space, so it may be wise to take stock and look towards the future.

Collections

Whether you take an interest in geology, mineralogy or palaeontology depends partly on where you live and how much time can be spent in exploring mountains, quarries, road cuttings and abandoned mines. The true 'rockhound' finds happiness in clambering about with a geological hammer and taking home heavy bags full of stones. Collecting very soon becomes compulsive as new specimens are found or purchased, but a collection of minerals or fossils needs to be properly housed and the question of display and storage soon becomes acute.

Keeping specimens wrapped up in newspaper in boxes is not satisfactory; they need to be set out in shallow trays, and the most prized deserve a lighted display cabinet. If there is no space for keeping a collection of hand specimens, there is fortunately an excellent alternative in making a collection of micro mounts. These are very small specimens kept in transparent boxes no more than 2.5 cm (1 in) square. A really important collection of micro mounts will fit into a small office filing cabinet. The only snag about micro mounts is that a binocular microscope

Fig. 30 Collection of hand specimens stored in shallow trays

is almost a necessity to make the most of them. Under high magnification minerals reveal striking beauty of colour and form which can be further exploited by fixing a camera to the microscope and making colour slides.

The advantage of micro mounts is that a small bag of rocks resulting from an expedition will provide many evenings of interesting exploration under the microscope looking for treasures which were not apparent in the field.

Collections tend towards specialization, such as all the minerals in one particular area or all members of one chemical group, so there will inevitably be rare specimens which have no great appeal to the eye. The lapidary is more concerned with the beauty of minerals and tends to collect clusters of crystals or pieces of natural beauty which are too good to be cut. Apart from this, most lapidaries cannot resist acquiring a stock of cutting material which soon becomes more than they can possibly cut in a lifetime.

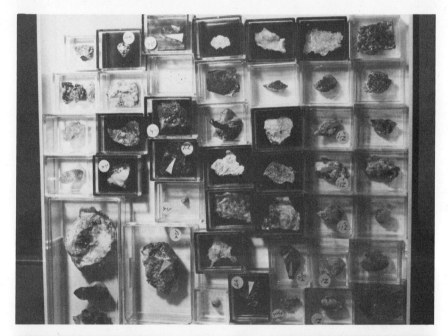

Fig. 31 Micro mounts stored in a filing cabinet

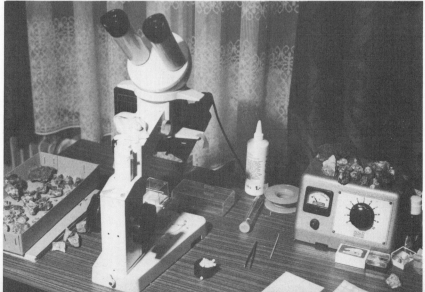

Fig. 32 Binocular microscope with spotlight attachment; the box of specimens will provide entertainment for many evenings

45

Organization

If lapidary work becomes paramount, and working gemstones takes precedence over collecting specimens, the ultimate development will be a permanent workshop fitted with lighting, heating, water and power supply for all kinds of machines. This possibility is not open to everybody and it even has drawbacks; there are keen lapidaries with workshops in the garden or the cellar who do not work in the winter because it is too cold, so there is something to be said for working by hand in a warm kitchen in the winter and enjoying expeditions during the summer.

Quite remarkable results can be had from hand working with a minimum of equipment, and this can even be done in a small flat; in fact all the supplies and apparatus mentioned in this book, the pebble polisher, flat laps, hand wheel, bench hook and faceting unit, plus all the associated bits and pieces, can be stowed into a space no bigger than a medium sized television set.

Organization and discipline are important because a working lapidary is a member of a community which has the right not to be incommoded. Peace in any home will be destroyed if a few principles are not observed, the first being that old-fashioned precept 'a place for everything and everything in its place'. The most practical room for working stones is the kitchen, but lapidary work and food preparation do not mix, and there can be no overlapping, therefore a time must be selected by mutual agreement when the lapidary can have an uninterrupted run of a couple of hours. At the end of that time all equipment must be put away in its proper place and any mess (and there will always be some mess) cleared up without trace.

Fig. 34 All the supplies and apparatus mentioned in this book can be stacked together in a space measuring 66 x 35 x 44 cm (26 x 14 x 17 in); note the plate glass faceting laps on shelves in a cardboard box

Grits stored in tins or jars should not be kept on kitchen shelves but elsewhere because it is too easy to mistake aluminium oxide for flour or salt. Of course, in fine weather the hand worker, being independent of electricity, can take his work out of doors, even into a beach hut or a boat.

Faceting

There is a special attraction about faceting because the equipment needed is light and relatively silent and there is very little mess. One can work in a living room with either a hand unit or a normal faceting machine and the working space need be no more than that required to write a letter. The one necessity is good lighting. It is worth while examining the possibility of short circuiting the usual progression to faceting through cabochon making, and go straight into faceting—and beginning with a hand unit is a simple and inexpensive introduction.

Output

There are hobbies such as painting and pottery where the quantity of the finished product soon becomes a problem, and this is true to a lesser extent with stones, but the output of a hand worker is not likely to cause much embarrassment.

As soon as they are shown a pretty cabochon or a faceted gem, most people immediately react in the same way and say, 'You could sell it'. Presumably the thought process is that an uncommon skill must be exploited for profit. The lapidary may think otherwise; if he or she has spent a long time making a beautiful object why should it be sold to someone else, unless the wolf is actually breaking down the door? Surely there is more satisfaction to be had from building up a unique collection of unusual and beautiful finished gems than in selling them for a little money.

Make no mistake, in spite of some advertisments, the money will not be big money and no amateur can compete with professional cutters working commercially, especially those in developing countries who toil for scant reward. If the hobby is looked upon as a money spinner it will soon lose its attraction, on the other hand if friends really want to buy a piece for their own use, this can be a means for financing your own activity. The point to watch is that the tail does not wag the dog and an absorbing hobby be turned into a production-line drudgery.

Jewellery

One obvious outlet for finished stones is to make jewellery and there are many lapidaries who do this. Stones cut to conventional sizes with a template can be fitted into ready-made silver mountings. The lapidary who learns silversmithing as well has greater opportunity to experiment with unusual minerals and shapes such as are never to be seen in shops. When one person has mastered both crafts the scope for original design is immense, but silversmithing is outside the scope of this book, and there are plenty of good books on the subject.

Nevertheless the lapidary is bound to take a keen interest in any jewellery incorporating stones, and the simplest approach is to look in shop windows. It soon becomes apparent that antique jewellery is much more interesting than modern factory work, which is no more than precision engineering in precious metal with the addition of stones cut to standard sizes and shapes. The most interesting modern work is the 'one off' unique pieces made by individual craftsmen, but even these are not necessarily masterpieces.

Faceted stones can be extremely beautiful as well as valuable, and there is great variety in cut and shape. Faceting cuts seem to be subject to both fashion and tradition and the availability of opaque stones cut into cabochons depends somewhat on the political situation in the countries of origin, as well as new finds in the mines which may start a new fashion. On the whole the jewellery trade plays safe and offers the public familiar stones with a pedigree. It is easier to sell malachite, tiger-eye, or lapis-lazuli than an unusual stone with a strange name.

The lesson here is that the amateur should not spend his time doing what everybody else is doing but should search out little known materials, cut them into original shapes, and produce unique gems once the craft has been acquired with run-of-the-mill minerals. If you are to spend several hours faceting a gem, it does not make sense to work with commonplace quartz instead of something with far better qualities of refraction and dispersion which will give a much more brilliant finished piece.

In this connection it is not difficult to make your own index dials for a hand faceting unit which will differ from the 96 or 84 index dials used on machines. A little elementary geometry will produce dials for cutting stones with 5, 7 or 9 sides instead of the multiples of eight, and there are some who believe that stones with an odd number of main facets have a special brilliance not seen in those with matching pairs. In any case it is rare to see such stones offered for sale.

Those with experience of working stones with modern tools and abrasives cannot fail to be amazed at the skill and patience of the workers of antiquity. Museums and art collections display examples of delicate intaglio work or cameos made thousands of years ago. One is fascinated by the carved and polished treasures passed down from ancient civilizations in China, Egypt, Latin America or the Near East, as well as medieval work from Europe. To quote but one example, the cloisonné garnets to be seen in the Sutton Hoo treasure at the British Museum in London are a supreme instance of superb lapidary technique. In contrast there are crown jewels and ecclesiastical treasures set with crude lumps of coloured stone which the craftsmen of the time did not know how to cut and polish.

The point I wish to make is that the amateur should strive to break away from the commonplace and produce original work of real artistic merit, and that inspiration can be had from studying the masterpieces of antiquity, although everything old is not a masterpiece. Need it be said that all these treasures were made by hand and not with machines?

Counting the cost

Photography and hi-fi music are relatively expensive hobbies, where the amount involved can be divided between the initial cost of basic equipment and the running costs of films, records, cassettes and so on. Before becoming more deeply committed to lapidary work, it will be prudent to look at the costings. There is practically no limit to what can be spent on capital equipment, and if a proper workshop is fitted out with slab saw, trim saw, vibrating laps and tumblers, diamond grinding wheels, drills and polishing pads, plus a first class faceting unit, the cost can easily run into thousands of pounds or dollars.

Happily there are two other courses open, the first of which is to make one's own apparatus for working stones by hand, in which case the expense will be minimal. It is within reach of young people from the age of ten upwards who receive normal pocket money, or it can be managed by a retired man or woman looking for a new hobby which will not overstrain a reduced income.

In this case the most costly item is the bench grinder plus lapidary grinding wheels, but even this will not amount to more than the price of an ordinary pair of shoes. There are a number of miscellaneous items, wood and glass for making different pieces of apparatus, a magnifying glass or jeweller's loupe, a spirit lamp, a small hack saw and various nuts and bolts, nails and glue, but none of these items are as costly as cameras or tuners. Next come the expendables—abrasive papers, loose grits, polishing powders, epoxy resin, dopwax and so forth—but these will last a long time and their cost cannot compare with films or cassettes.

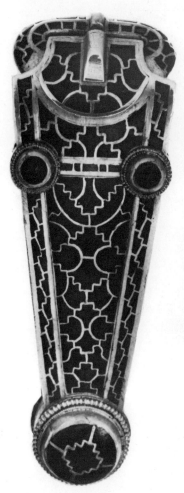

Fig. 35 Cloisonné garnets cut to complex and intricate shapes. Anglo Saxon work of the 7th century from the Sutton Hoo ship burial (courtesy of the British Museum)

Lastly there is the raw material for cutting, and this needs watching carefully. There is a big difference in price for the same thing between one supplier and another and it pays to shop around, or write for catalogues if a visit is impossible, and compare prices for equal quality. Obviously if you are going to spend a good deal of time and effort on working gemstones by hand it does not make sense to buy low grade material except for practising.

The handworker is especially interested in minerals which have been sliced, and these fetch a higher price than rough, whole nodules. This is comparable to buying the best fillets of steak or fish; you get the best part of the stone, but the off-cuts and nubs have to be paid for somehow, so the higher prices for a slice may not be so high after all.

Handwork being a slow process, the total amount of raw material needed will not be great, and the cost is easily kept within bounds. However if you decide you prefer cutting opal, then the price will begin to rise enormously, but faceting-grade aquamarine or garnet is reasonable in price and will cut excellent gems. Remember too that a finished gem is more valuable than the original piece it was cut from in spite of considerable loss in weight.

Between a fully equipped workshop and simple hand gear lies a middle way which may be the best solution for most people; it is to buy a combination machine which has a trim saw and a grinding unit and to mount it on top of the driving motor so that the whole thing can be moved about and stowed away when not in use. These versatile machines when used in conjunction with flat laps and a faceting unit, hand or otherwise, bring every aspect of lapidary work within reach of an amateur. The prices of these machines can be had from suppliers' catalogues and advertisements in the magazines. However there is every reason to make a start with handwork before buying a machine because the necessary gear, including the hand wheel, will still come in useful and will not be wasted. The hand wheel is especially useful for polishing because of its slower speed with infinite control. It can also be carried about and is ideal for use in a caravan.

Money will be needed to buy a few good reference books; an illustrated guide to minerals and rocks, an elementary book on geology, a map of mineral sites throughout the country and a manual on faceting or general lapidary technique. A subscription to at least one magazine is necessary because these provide useful information about clubs, dealers, exhibitions and shows, as well as interesting articles.

It is not suggested that all these things have to be bought before starting to work; they can be acquired progressively and some of them are suitable for birthday or Christmas presents. The total cost of everything needed for pebble polishing and flat lapping, including random faceting, is very small and no obstacle to anyone who would like to make a start. The next step which involves buying a bench grinder is a little more serious but it is a commitment which cannot be considered costly. The real break comes when a change is made from hand to machine work and even at this stage the knowledge acquired by hand working is invaluable for choosing the right machine and not being sold something unsuitable.

Lapidary clubs

Although they are not common, there are lapidary clubs spread about the country, and there are also some schools where the subject is taught. If there is a possibility of joining a club it should be done, because then there will be opportunities to learn from more experienced people and also, perhaps, to have the occasional use of club machinery for preparing material.

Club membership could be increased if more people take up working by hand. For example when a cabochon has been ground to shape there is no need to use a machine for the sanding and polishing which can be done perfectly well on a hand wheel. Hand wheels are light enough to be brought to club meetings and taken home again, and this arrangement would free valuable machine time for sawing and essential grinding so that more people can be working at any one time. The same arrangement might be helpful in schools when the budget has been cut and there are not enough machines to go round. A competent faceter could give instruction to a small class of people each working with a home-made faceting unit, and a club machine could soon make a few pre-forms.

If joining a club is out of the question it is still a good idea to try to work with others rather than by oneself. Two friends can pool resources and share materials as well as exchanging ideas and information. With a hand wheel they can take it in turns to supply the motive power so that two hands can be used instead of one to hold the work. If others can be persuaded to join in, a new club can be founded.

Recycling materials

In order to keep down costs every effort should be made to make use of all the things which our consumer society is so ready to throw away. Recycling town rubbish is very much in fashion, and it must appeal to anybody who feels that the natural resources of the world should not be wasted. In case the lapidary begins to worry about cutting up rocks the mineral deposits which are known today are capable of supplying enormous quantities of all the popular stones in demand, and the amount of quartz used by lapidaries is insignificant compared to the needs of industry.

Lapidaries can make good use of felt, leather, rubber and some plastics, and very often pieces large enough to provide polishing pads and discs can be cut from discarded handbags, boots and hats, although felt may need steaming to make it lie flat. An abandoned raincoat will make several pebble polishers, and plastic bottles have all sorts of uses from funnels to containers. Most of them are thermoplastic, which means that they soften when carefully heated near a flame and go hard again when cool, so their original shape can be modified. A sump for a hand wheel is easily made like this.

Polystyrene (or styrofoam) is very versatile, especially if it is the close-grained sort that does not crumble easily. Radio shops throw away the packaging made from polystyrene. It is easily cut with a sharp knife moistened with water and detergent, and hollows can be made with a hot wire.

Thin slats of wood for polishing laps are to be had from the wooden crates used for fruit and lettuce. Salvage plate glass has already been mentioned.

When using a geological hammer for smashing rocks it is absolutely necessary to have some kind of protection for the eyes against flying splinters. A sheet of clear plastic with an elastic fastening can take the place of goggles and it takes up less room in one's pocket.

Beware of false economies and always buy the best quality you can afford when the grade of the equipment matters. Do not throw away sanding discs too readily, because a worn 220 grit is the equivalent of a much finer grade and can be used as such. On the other hand, ungraded loose grits are a bad buy and it does not pay to use grit when it has become muddy and has lost its bite. Polishing powders should be used very sparingly and washed off frequently to make room for a fresh layer. If polish is allowed to build up round the edge of a flat lap, it is certain to produce unwanted scratches.

The idea is to look round the house before buying anything new, to see whether there is something unwanted which will serve the purpose. This can save money which the hobbyist can then put to better use. There is no need to go to extremes like the lady with a box for 'Pieces of string too short to be of use'.

6 ABRASIVES AND POLISHES

Silicon carbide

Until the end of the nineteenth century lapidaries had to be content with what abrasives could be found in nature; sharp sand, powdered garnet, tripoli, emery and diamond—and it is remarkable what beautiful and intricately worked pieces they managed to produce. Tripoli, sometimes called rotten-stone, is a kind of earth formed by decomposing siliceous minerals and it has a hardness of 7 on Mohs' scale; it is sold in cake form for polishing metals. Emery is a natural product, being a granular form of the mineral corundum mixed with iron oxide, and as corundum is the hardest of all minerals except diamond, emery was widely used before the arrival of modern synthetic abrasives.

In 1891 an American called Acheson used a powerful electric current to fuse a mixture of coke and sand, and he obtained silicon carbide. A few years later another American, using a similar process, produced synthetic aluminium oxide. These new synthetic abrasives revolutionized the lapidary profession and made it possible for amateurs to enter the field. Up to that time the knowledge of how to work gemstones was confined to a few professionals who jealously guarded their secrets.

When Dr Acheson first made silicon carbide he thought he had made synthetic corundum and he coined the word 'carborundum' for his product. This name later became a trademark and it is often used now for silicon carbide grindstones, in much the same way as a vacuum flask is called a thermos. Today, silicon carbide has largely replaced natural materials for making grinding wheels and for coating paper and cloth; it is also sold in the form of loose grit. As it is cheap, and will cut everything except diamond, it is a boon to lapidaries both professional and amateur.

Grinding wheels, coated papers and loose grits are all made in various grades of coarseness identified by a number which represents the size of the mesh used to screen the powder. Grit labelled 100 will have passed through a sieve with 100 meshes to the linear inch (2.5 cm), but when it comes to the finer grades 400, 600 or less, then a mesh cannot be used, and separation is carried out by other methods. Nevertheless the series of numbers representing mesh is still used, and a tube of diamond compound may well be described as being 30,000 mesh equivalent.

Grindstones

A hand worker can make good use of two kinds of grindstone, flat and circular. The kind of flat stone sold for sharpening garden tools is very useful when used in the same way as a file, and a circular grindstone is essential when using a bench grinder to make cabochons. A stone of around 100 grit will quickly remove surplus material, and one of 220 will give a smoother finish and be less likely to cause chipping round the edge of the stone being ground, but there is another factor to be taken into account.

Grinding wheels are made of particles of silicon carbide of uniform size bonded together by other substances with the result that some wheels are denser than others. There is a grading system to identify the density or hardness of a wheel and dealers will advise on which is the best wheel for any particular purpose. For hand working a soft stone is better, because paradoxically a soft grindstone will cut hard minerals faster than a hard one. This is because the hard stone is denser and so the mineral tends to skid over the surface and remain untouched; it can be compared to what happens in flat lapping. Fresh grit stays as separate grains and cuts rapidly but as it mixes with powdered mineral it forms a much denser slurry and the cutting action slows up. This is why a flat lap should be frequently cleaned and loaded with fresh grit, and a grinding wheel must have a good supply of water to swill away the sludge and retain maximum cutting efficiency.

It is best to have two wheels, one of 100 and one of 220 grit, but if only one can be afforded the coarser one should have priority. When buying wheels make sure that they will fit the arbor of your bench grinder and buy a bush if necessary.

Grits

A good selection of grit sizes, whether loose or bonded to paper or cloth is coarse (100) medium (220/300) and fine (400/600) and if a stone is sanded progressively with these three grades it will be fit for polishing. However as has already been explained, the action of loose grit is different from that of paper or cloth and so the fine grade of silicon carbide should

Fig. 36 Silicon carbide made into grindstones, coated paper and loose grit

be followed by aluminium oxide. It is a matter of personal choice whether to use paper or cloth; cloth is more expensive but more durable, and well worn cloths are often very useful for polishing difficult stones. In each case the sheets must be waterproof for lapidary work. They measure 28 × 23 cm (11 × 9 in.) and it is just possible to cut two 15 cm (6 in) diameter discs from a sheet, which is normally an economy.

Abrasive compounds and polishes have to be of uniform quality. The purpose of sanding with a fine abrasive is to remove the scratches made by a previous coarser one, and if the abrasive is not of uniform quality this will not be done. Moreover if care is not taken to avoid contamination and a few grains are carried over from the previous step there will be unwanted scratches which will spoil the finish. In practice this means washing stones, hands and dopstick at each stage, making sure that there are no grains under fingernails or in cracks in the stone which will cause trouble. Water bottles and sponges must be kept clean too.

When grits are stored in covered jars the size should be clearly written on the lid as well as on the jar. Flat sheets are best kept between the pages of an old magazine. All this may sound unnecessarily fussy, but much time spent in preparing a fine finish on a stone can be sacrificed by a little carelessness and the work must be done over again.

Diamond

There is an alternative to using silicon carbide and that is to use powdered diamond. Diamond-impregnated grinding wheels cut far faster than silicon carbide ones, and diamond compound used on laps also speeds up the sanding and polishing processes. The main drawback to using diamond is its high initial cost, but as very little is needed and the work proceeds much more quickly there are some who maintain that in the long run diamond may even be more economical in use than conventional abrasives. The beginner will use silicon carbide, but the possibility of switching over should be borne in mind. The cost can be worked out fairly accurately by referring to prices in dealers' catalogues, but it will not be justified unless there is a fairly large production from hard material.

Before diamond saws came on the market, lapidaries used what is known as a 'mud saw', which was either a metal disc or a long wire which moved against the stone in a mixture of grit and water which slowly cut it. Although the idea may have its attraction there is little to be gained in playing about with mud saws today. Diamond-impregnated metal drills are useful for making small holes to mount a stone as a pendant or earring and these can be used in an ordinary drill. They are not too high in price and are much better than drilling with a tube of copper and silicon carbide grit.

Polishes

Except for diamond all the polishing powders in common use happen to be metallic oxides of tin, cerium, chrome, aluminium and iron, and they have two properties in common, they are all hard and they have high melting points. Recipes for polishing stones are like those for mixing cocktails, each adept having his own preferences and secret formulae. Some combinations have proved their efficacy and are in general use for particular stones, but results depend not only on the polish but also on the lap used with it. Stationary or rotating laps can be made from felt, leather, wood, plastic, metal, cloth or even wax. The addition of detergent, softening rinse, or vinegar is common to improve the finish.

Occasionally books and magazines refer to polishing with oxalic acid, which in solid form is a white powder looking like common salt. It has the disadvantage of being extremely poisonous and the amateur will do well to have nothing to do with it. There is serious risk of an accident if oxalic acid is taken into a kitchen and there are other agents which will polish soft stones just as well if not better.

Of the well known successful combinations tin oxide used on a felt lap will produce a brilliant polish on agates and similar hard material. Cerium oxide is now widely used instead of tin oxide, which has risen steeply in price. I have been using cerium oxide on a lap of soft PVC sheet with great success for all kinds of quartz as well as other hard minerals. The heat build-up is very rapid and care is necessary not to overheat. There is nothing to be gained by using too much polish on a lap, and in the case of cerium oxide on a flat sheet of PVC, the amount which can be carried in three or four dabs of a loaded water-colour brush is enough. The polish is spread over the lap with a finger tip which easily detects any particles which need to be removed.

Tin or cerium oxide on a felt lap do nothing for malachite, which responds well to a thick slurry of chrome oxide on a leather lap. Lapis-lazuli can also be polished in the same way, but chrome oxide is unpopular because it makes such a terrible mess. It is bright green and stains everything it touches as well as creeping into crevices where it cannot be dislodged. A cleaner alternative is Linde A on leather or wood. There can be no hard and fast rules about polishing and if one combination fails to bring results another may act like magic. For this reason it is advisable to keep a notebook and log successful and unsuccessful techniques for future reference. Some workers even use two different polishes on the same lap.

Polishing powders are normally sold loose but there is a firm which makes them up into a stick about the same size as a stick of shaving soap and this can be very convenient.

It is easy to overlook the kind of water one uses for polishing. Water from the tap may contain minute particles of sand or lime coarser than the polishing powder in use. A special water bottle should be kept for polishing, and this can be filled either with distilled water, or water melted from the ice which collects inside the cold compartment of an ordinary refrigerator.

There are different theories about what happens to a stone when the surface takes on a polish and this was not accurately determined until the advent of the electron microscope. What is quite certain is that a good polish cannot be obtained at all unless the surface is properly prepared first.

7 DOPPING

Dopping is the term used for fixing a stone firmly to a short handle so that it can be more easily manipulated. In the initial stages of grinding a cabochon, it is best to hold a stone in the fingers, but for doming, sanding and polishing, the work is easier if the stone is dopped. The traditional way of dopping is to use a special wax which is much like sealing wax, and a short length of wood dowelling. Dopsticks come in different sizes but a good length is 10 or 12.5 cm (4 or 5 in) long and 1 cm ($\frac{1}{2}$ in) in diameter. Dopwax is melted and moulded round the end of the stick and the stone, which also has to be heated, is then embedded in the wax. There are some amateur lapidaries who do not like dopping, they find it difficult to do; they burn their fingers, stones refuse to stick or fall off later in the middle of grinding, and tempers become frayed.

Every lapidary should learn the standard technique of dopping with wax because sometimes there is no alternative, but there are other ways of doing the job using modern adhesives and some of the difficulties of conventional dopping can be side-stepped. In the chapter on pebble polishing it was suggested that pebbles be stuck to corks with quick-setting epoxy resin and this technique can be further exploited.

Fig. 37 Stones dopped with wax on wooden sticks in the conventional way

Conventional dopping

Dopwax, dopsticks and a spirit lamp (or tablets of Meta fuel) are needed for this. A candle can be used but smoke from the flame causes trouble and any kind of smokeless flame is better. First of all one needs to find out whether the stone can stand up to being heated, as many stones crack or discolour when heated and they have to be dopped another way. It saves time to assemble a number of stones for a dopping session and so a good stock of dopsticks of different sizes should be built up.

If a stone is greasy or dirty it will not stick well to the dopwax so begin by thoroughly cleaning the stones with detergent and perhaps wiping them with a cloth dipped in acetone. After this do not touch the surface which is to be stuck with your fingers; this is specially important if the stone has already been half polished and the polished surface is to be gripped by dopwax.

Stones are heated up slowly and this can be done on top of an empty tin can with a hole cut in the side and a source of heat underneath. Single stones can be heated up in an old spoon held over a flame. The stones are

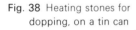

Fig. 38 Heating stones for dopping, on a tin can

Fig. 39 The stone on the right is incorrectly dopped, it does not sit squarely on the dopstick

at the right heat when a small piece of wax pressed against them begins to melt, and when this happens the heat source must be removed. While the stones are warming up, dopwax is softened near a flame and the end of a dopstick is covered with it and formed into an inverted cone. Hot wax does not stick to cold surfaces so the wax can be formed by rolling it along a cold surface of metal or glass. It is also moulded to shape with wet fingers so a bowl of cold water must be close at hand. Dopwax has a nasty habit of melting and drops fall on the little finger of the hand holding the stone unless it is tucked firmly out of the way. If the wax is overheated or if it catches fire it will lose its grip.

When a cone has been built up on the end of the stick the top is flattened by pressing it against something cold and then melted slightly ready to receive the hot stone. The two are pressed firmly together and wax is built up with the fingers round the base of the stone, but not too far. Ideally the stone should be fixed centrally and squarely on the dopstick. The difficulty for beginners is to have everything in the right place before the wax sets, and usually the wax has to be held near the flame once more so that adjustments can be made. If all goes well the dop should be put on one side until everything has cooled down. It is very much a question of more haste less speed, and if grinding the stone begins before the wax has properly set the stone will come off the dop and the work has to be done over again.

Common faults are having the stone more to one side than the other, or having it tilted in relation to the stick, and if the stone is left like this all the subsequent shaping and finishing will be much more difficult to do and there is a good chance that the finished stone will be lop-sided. It pays to

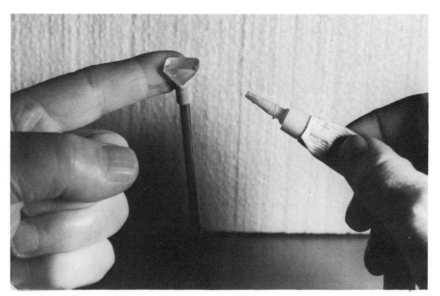

Fig. 40 An unpleasant thing to
happen

do the dopping properly before moving on. Another fault is to build up too much wax round the base of the stone in which case it will be in the way when grinding and it also prevents the worker from seeing where the edge of the stone is. Surplus wax can quickly be trimmed off with a knife.

Pebbles can be dopped onto corks with dopwax instead of epoxy resin. Stones dopped in this way are easily taken off the dop by putting them to soak in a glass of water with crushed ice. If any traces of wax stick to the stone they can be dissolved in alcohol.

This method cannot be used for stones which are sensitive to heat and the alternative suggested in most instructions on dopping is to use a dough made from acetone glue and cornflour. In practice this method does not work well, especially on polished surfaces, and the stones come off, but fortunately there are better ways using modern adhesives. Two adhesives are useful for dopping, epoxy resin and alpha cyanocrylate, both of which were discussed in the chapter on pebble polishing. Great care is necessary when handling the alpha glue because it sticks to the skin and it is not pleasant to find a stone firmly dopped on one's finger tip, a disaster which can happen in a matter of seconds.

One way to dop a heat-sensitive stone is to prepare a dopstick and wax in the usual way and then quickly press the stone into the wax while it is soft and pull it away immediately. When the wax sets stick the stone in place with one or two drops of alpha glue. To get it off the dop most of the wax can be removed with a hot knife blade and the remains scraped off or dissolved. This is a good method if the base of the stone is not flat, but for making cabochons there is considerable advantage to be gained by making a set of metal dops, and this is not difficult.

Big nails and flat headed bolts and screws can all be used as dops for small stones, but for cabochons ideal dops can soon be made from nuts and bolts and an off-cut of sheet aluminium. Buy a few bolts with a flat, countersunk head and two nuts for each one, a good size is 5 cm (2 in) long by 4 mm ($\frac{3}{16}$ in) diameter—as they come. The aluminium strip needs to be thick enough to take the bolt-head so that it lies flat with the surface in a hole which has to be countersunk; about 3 mm ($\frac{1}{8}$ in) will suffice, and this thickness of metal is easily cut with a small hack saw and drilled by hand. The dops shown here were made from the same aluminium strip as the splashguard for the hand wheel. There is no need to go to the trouble of making oval dops because hexagons or rectangles with the corners off give quite sufficient support.

It is worth while spending some time on making a selection of different sized dops out of aluminium, and when you are quite sure that the hole is in the centre and the countersink deep enough to take the head, the bolt is put through the hole and a nut put underneath and screwed up tight. A second nut is threaded on the bolt about half way up. Each of these little metal dops is now screwed into a hole just the right size in a piece of wooden dowelling 10 cm (4 in) long and the second nut screwed tight up against the end of the dowelling to prevent further movement. The hole in the wood may need packing to secure the thread of the bolt, and about half the length of the bolt should be embedded inside the dowelling, but do not glue it in place.

The result is a dopstick which handles just like a conventional one but there is no longer any problem about making sure that the stone is quite square on the stick. Alternative handles for the dops can be lengths of bamboo cane with a hole the right size, or ready-made handles for small tools which can be bought cheaply.

Fig. 41 Sheet aluminium and two dops made from it with nuts and bolts. Also a dop made from a piece of Meccano (toy construction kit) and a tool handle

Stones are attached to the aluminium dop with wax or with epoxy resin or alpha glue. When using wax the bolt can be partly unscrewed from the handle so that the latter does not burn. If a large enough dop is chosen, only a very thin coating of wax is needed for a firm bond, and the edge of the stone is left free.

Epoxy resin or alpha glue can be used instead of wax and they make an even firmer bond. All that is needed to remove the stone is to heat the dop until the glue gives way when the stone is twisted.

These metal dops are ideal for heat sensitive stones and there are two variations for fixing them. Small stones can be glued directly to the metal and when it is time to take them off the dop is unscrewed from the handle and stone and dop are immersed in a small, covered jar of acetone until the glue dissolves, which may be several hours. Larger stones are best attached in another way; first the metal dop is given a coating of epoxy resin and when hard it is rubbed down to a flat surface with a file or abrasive paper, leaving a thickness of under 1 mm ($\frac{1}{32}$ in) or the thickness of a thumbnail. The stone is then dopped to this layer with fresh epoxy and left to set. To remove it the stone is simply cut away from the dop with a fine hacksaw blade or a jeweller's saw, there being enough clearance between the metal and the stone for the blade to pass without damaging the stone. Surplus glue sticking to the stone can be scraped or dissolved off.

This method is excellent for transfer dopping stones during faceting and there is less chance of a stone breaking loose than when wax is used. To save on epoxy resin it is advisable to prepare one or two dops with a first coating whenever epoxy has been used for some job and there is some left over.

Instead of cutting them out from aluminium strip, another way to make metal dops is to silver solder small coins to flat-headed screws, which are

Fig. 42 Removing a stone from a metal dop by soaking it in acetone

Fig. 43 A jeweller's saw is a useful tool especially when transfer dopping

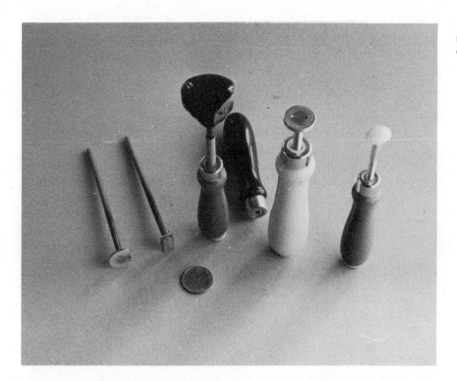

Fig. 44 Metal dops can be made from nails, screws, bolts, coins, washers etc

then screwed into wooden handles, but the coin will have to be filed down flat on the working face. A big stone can be dopped on a 2.5 cm (1 in) pulley wheel (taken from a toy meccano set) screwed to a length of axle rod. In dopping, as in all processes, there is plenty of opportunity to use one's ingenuity and take advantage of anything useful.

The metal dops recommended here make dopping much easier than conventional dopping, and many lapidaries will welcome the chance to have less to do with spirit lamps and burnt fingers; nevertheless old-fashioned dopwax is often quite the best way of doing special jobs.

8 PLAY OF LIGHT

The lapidary cuts and polishes gemstones to make them appear more beautiful than they are in their natural state and to show off any special characteristics they may have. In the case of a pebble or any other opaque stone the most that can be done is to polish the surface so that as much light as possible is reflected from it. The colour and marking of a stone so polished will be enhanced because more of the light falling on it is reflected back to the eye of the beholder.

A rough surface is one where a series of irregular ridges and hollows absorb light or scatter it in all directions so that the stone looks dull and lifeless. If the stone is wet or if the hollows and ridges are removed by grinding and polishing, much more light is reflected to the eye and the stone is seen in all its beauty. This is what happens when a stone, such as a piece of malachite, is cut into a cabochon. The stone does not normally have any special optical properties and the markings are made to stand out simply by producing a very smooth surface.

There are many minerals with a particular atomic structure that alters the play of any light falling on them to produce a whole range of optical phenomena including double refraction, lustre, chatoyancy, schiller, asterism, opalescence and iridescence. The art of the lapidary lies in knowing how to take advantage of these special properties and use them to produce the most beautiful gem possible.

The lustre or sheen of an opaque stone depends on reflected light coming from the surface and not from any penetration. Lustre is infinitely variable, as can be seen from the objects around us; the lustre of polished silver is a metallic one differing from that of a wine glass, a pearl or glossy paint. The lustre seen by the eye enables the brain to assess what things are made of, so that without touching them we can note the difference between an enamel bath and a porcelain basin. The hard lustre of diamond is said to be adamantine whereas that of moonstone is better described as silky. Lustre can be pearly, vitreous, waxy, greasy or silky; everything which shines in bright light has its own special lustre.

Minerals which are translucent offer different effects as some of the light penetrates below the surface and is reflected back from minute tubes or particles inside the stone. A particularly striking effect is that of iridescence in precious opal, so called to distinguish it from ordinary opal which has only a uniform milky appearance. Precious opal displays brilliant flashes of 'fire' covering the whole spectrum of the rainbow. It is this 'fire' which makes opal so much sought after and so expensive, and it is due to the internal structure of the stone where minute particles split up the rays of white light and reflect its coloured components back to the eye.

Great care is needed when working opal because it is all too easy to grind the layers where the fire originates and then the whole effect disappears. What the lapidary does is to remove as much surplus material as he dare, leaving the fire close to the surface of the finished stone, so achieving maximum brilliance. Opal is not a stone for beginners, it is something to look forward to with pleasurable anticipation.

Several minerals in the feldspar group have a characteristic play of light known as a 'schiller'. In the case of labradorite, for example, the stone is greyish and not very interesting when viewed from some angles, but suddenly in one position the light is reflected back from an internal layer in a sheet of brilliant colour. It may be blue, green or gold and it has the same kind of luminosity as the wings of tropical butterflies. A thin sheet of labradorite when seen against the light can be almost transparent, yet when it is turned to another angle the coloured schiller appears as if by magic. Moonstones and sunstones also from the feldspar group show a floating blue or white lustre when correctly cut. Light entering the stone is reflected back from a mass of minute parallel tubes and a silky flash seems to hover over the surface of the stone when it is tilted. The way to cut cabochons correctly from these stones is described later on.

Chatoyancy is yet another optical effect easily seen in tiger-eye agate, a mineral having parallel, fibrous layers which give it a silky look. When a piece of tiger-eye is rotated, bands which first appear as dark brown change to golden yellow, and vice-versa. The lapidary takes advantage of this phenomenon when he cuts a cabochon so that a band of light flashes across the surface at right angles to the direction of the internal fibres.

There are forms of quartz, including rose quartz, where the growth of the original crystal took place in such a way that light reflected from inside appears as a star on the surface of a cut stone. This is known as asterism and it can be seen in some rubies and sapphires, both of which consist mainly of corundum. Occasionally the mineral corundum contains minute traces of other substances which render it slightly opaque and when a crystal of corundum forms in the earth's crust it is invariably six-sided, and any inclusions will also line up in layers or masses conforming to the overall hexagonal shape. The lapidary takes a good look to determine where the optical axis of the crystal lies and he cuts his stone with the base at right angles to this axis. The inclusions then radiate round this axis like the spokes of a wheel, and light reflected from them forms a star with six rays.

If a piece of asteroid material is cut into a spherical bead there will be a star on top and a similar one on the bottom. If the bead is then cut in half through the equator the result will be two perfect 'star' cabochons. If it is cut through the poles the cabochons will have only cat's-eyes instead of stars. This illustrates the importance of orienting rough correctly before cutting.

Beginners are advised to save up any star sapphires they may have until later on, but tiger-eye agate, labradorite and moonstone are not expensive and they are excellent material for experimenting with as soon as the basic technique has been mastered.

There is a thing called the optical axis of a crystal which has to be taken into account when dealing with minerals which are dichroic or pleochroic, in other words minerals which change colour according to which way you look at them. Tourmaline is a good example of a dichroic mineral, and a crystal which appears a bright apple green sideways on immediately looks almost black from the end. Obviously this is important when a crystal of tourmaline is cut into a gem, and tourmaline is usually step cut parallel to its optical axis as this produces the best colour effect. A brilliant cut in the other direction would be too dark.

Cordierite (alias iolite) is an interesting dichroic mineral with three different colours. Cut into a cube it will look yellow, pale blue or violet according to which way it is turned. Among other places, cordierite is found in Finland and Norway and an interesting theory has been put forward that early Vikings used it as an aid to navigation taking advantage of its dichroism to determine the position of the sun even on cloudy days.

There is a very rare and costly variety of chrysoberyl called alexandrite which has a remarkable colour change from bright green in sunlight to red in artificial light. One is much more likely to come across synthetic alexandrite than the real thing, but the colour change is not so striking.

So far the different kinds of light play described have all depended on reflection, but where minerals are transparent refraction also adds to the effect, in both coloured and colourless stones. Good quality transparent minerals are not as a rule cut as cabochons, they are faceted, and the angles at which these facets are cut are very important, being calculated according to the refractive index of the mineral concerned to send back to the eye the maximum amount of light entering the gem. If a gem is cut with a flat 'table' at the top, any ray of light entering through the table bounces around inside the gem like the spot of light in a game played on a TV screen. If the facet angles of the bottom or pavilion part of the gem are wrong then the light goes out of play and is lost, with subsequent loss of brilliance. When the angles are right the ray rebounds from the surfaces of the facets and comes out through the table, and it is this which gives a gem its sparkle.

You can find lists giving the so-called critical angle for any transparent material and if the facets are cut at a lesser angle than this the light will escape and the gem will become what is popularly known as a 'fish-eye'. The critical angle is the dividing line between rays which are reflected from a surface and those which instead of being reflected pass through the surface and are bent as they pass from one medium to another. An example is the well-known effect of a stick which appears to be bent when it is put into a pool of water.

The scientific name for this bending is refraction and its importance for the lapidary is that the higher the refractive index of a transparent mineral the more flashes of colour will come from a faceted gem. White light entering the gem is split into all the colours of the rainbow just as a glass prism will produce bands of colour. The higher the refractive index of a substance and the greater the distance a ray of light travels inside a gem before coming out again, the more pronounced will be the flashes of colour produced by refraction. This is known as dispersion and it is the main reason why all imitation diamonds fail to compare with the real thing. A big diamond will show more colour than a small one because the light travels farther inside it, and the particular cut known as 'brilliant' is designed to take maximum advantage of these optical laws.

To sum up, a lapidary needs all the information he can obtain about the nature of a piece of rough before he starts work on it. It has to be correctly oriented and cut with precision to exhibit to the full the splendours offered by the optical peculiarities of any given piece. The exact chemical and physical composition of minerals and the laws governing their optical properties are all recent discoveries of modern science, and formerly lapidaries worked by trial and error. With our new knowledge, lapidary work becomes more precise, abrasives are chosen for specific operations, saws are lubricated, and polishes are related to different kinds of lap, but even so there is still room for trial and error because no two pieces of rough are exactly alike and every one presents a new challenge even to an experienced lapidary.

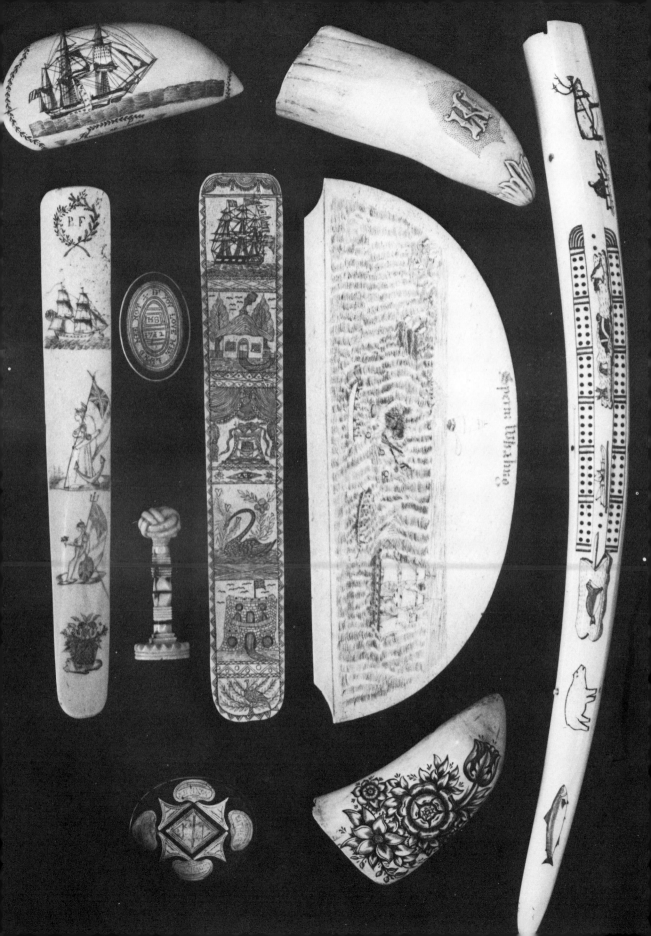

9 CARVING AND ENGRAVING

Organic materials

A lapidary, strictly speaking, is one who cuts, polishes or engraves precious stones, but there is no need to observe rigid demarcation lines when choosing a hobby. There are stones which are not precious, and organic materials which are not stones, such as shell, ivory, bone, jet, amber and coral, all of which are excellent for carving and polishing. The advantage of these organic materials is that they are not hard and can all be cut and shaped with hacksaws, files, drills and the kind of woodworking tools people use for odd jobs. There are also some very pretty minerals which can be worked in the same way.

Instead of, or as well as, working gemstones a lapidary may be drawn to making cameos from shell, etching scrimshaws, or carving jet and amber. An interesting hobby not widely practised today is etching or engraving glass with a diamond point. No tools are needed apart from the diamond graver and anyone who can do this well will find a demand for the finished article.

Scrimshaws

Scrimshaws have come back into fashion and more and more people are making them. Originally they were engravings on whale's tooth, walrus tusk or shell, done by sailors on whaling ships in the early nineteenth century. Intricate designs of ships, girls, flowers etc. were etched into the tusk or tooth with the point of a knife or a sail needle, after which they were blackened. Genuine, early scrimshaws are keenly sought by collectors at high prices, but new work is being produced today in material which varies from simple bone to fossilized mammoth ivory.

Cameo and intaglio

Carving and engraving can be divided into two sections, hard and soft. The handworker must necessarily confine himself to working in soft materials, unless he has infinite patience. There is a halfway house in the form of small power driven carving tools running on low voltage electricity. These extremely neat and versatile tools are no bigger than a can of beer and they can be held in the hand or clamped in different positions. To go with them

Fig. 45a Scrimshaw objects carved by whalers in the eighteenth century: the incised and inked drawings on the bones and teeth were mainly of nautical subjects, and were given or sold as momentos and souvenirs (courtesy City of Kingston upon Hull Maritime Museum)

Fig. 45b Detail of the scrimshaw tooth depicting a whaling ship

Fig. 45c Detail of the other side of the tooth showing the whalers harpooning a whale

Fig. 46 North American Indian shell disc (c AD 1000), about 8 cm (3 in) in diameter, showing the crested woodpeckers which guard the four directions that encircle the sun (courtesy Werner Forman Archive)

there is an enormous range of abrasive wheels, drills and carving points which will tackle hard stone.

If the piece of rough can be blanked out elsewhere it is quite feasible to carve small objects in the home provided some arrangement can be made for extracting the inevitable dust. With these tools one can carve cameos in real onyx or make netsuke or do intaglio work. Intaglio is the technique of cutting a design below the surface of the stone, in the manner of a signet ring, so that a positive relief is obtained when wax is pressed into it.

The Greeks and Romans cut splendid cameos in different kinds of banded agate, but today most cameos are carved from shell, and this is an occupation ideally suited for hand work, shells being soft enough to work with steel tools. A trial run to get the feel of cameo carving is easily arranged and it can be done by children. Mix some dark powdered paint with plaster of Paris and cast a disc in a soft plastic lid. When the plaster goes off, but before it dries out, pour a small pool of white plaster in the middle, about 4 mm ($\frac{1}{8}$ in) thick. When it has all set hard a cameo can be carved with the point of a penknife, or lino-cut tools, cutting away the white down as far as the coloured base.

Similarly, experimental intaglio designs can be cut in Perspex (or Lucite) and when seen from the opposite side they appear like frosted glass. Simple brooches can be made this way, and lapidary technique can be used to polish Perspex which has been cut. A little practice in this way is not time lost because the next step is to buy sections of conch or helmet shell and carve real cameos taking advantage of the natural layers of different colour in these shells. Details of how to carve cameos are given in books on the subject and a great deal can be learnt from studying fine specimens in museums and the windows of antique shops.

Shell

In addition to the shells used for cameos there are others with bright, mother-of-pearl colouring which are often made into jewellery. One of the most striking and colourful is the abalone, which is admirably suited for hand work, with one proviso. When it is cut or filed the dust produced is toxic and has most unpleasant effects if it is inhaled. The worker must wear a mask and arrange for good ventilation to remove the dust. Freshwater mussel shells have good colouring and they can sometimes be found on the shores of inland lakes.

Fig. 47 Two types of helmet shell of the kind used for cameos and an abalone shell on the left

Fig. 48 Mother-of-pearl earrings cut from the shell of a freshwater mussel

Fig. 49 Pieces of drift jet from Whitby, and a pendant carved from one of the pieces

Jet

Jet is a most agreeable substance for carving and even for faceting, but it is not too easy to obtain good quality, hard jet, the best of which comes from Whitby in Yorkshire. Spanish jet tends to be softer. Victorian jewellery in jet was fashionable for mourning, and the really fine pieces which turn up occasionally in antique shops fetch high prices. Jet is a kind of coal and the carver should insist on the hard variety because the soft kind breaks too easily. The word hard, in this instance is relative, because jet rates at no more than 3 on Mohs' scale, nevertheless it will take a superb polish.

All that is needed for carving jet is a jeweller's saw, a drill, a sharp knife and an assortment of needle files. It is better to use sandpaper and emery paper rather than silicon carbide for rubbing down jet. Pre-polishing is

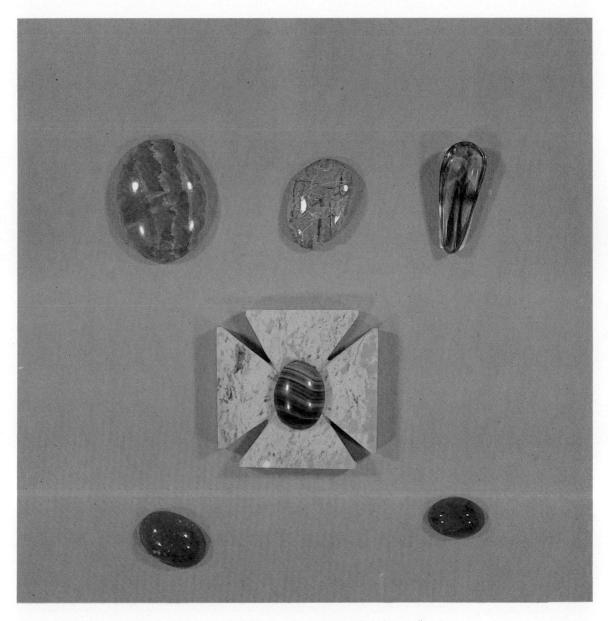

Cabochons and a Maltese Cross carved out on a bench hook: (top) amber, sodalite, chrysocolla, (centre) malachite on Connemara marble, (bottom) rhodochrosite, lapis lazuli

Beach pebbles and cabochons polished by hand

done with tripoli or aluminium oxide on chamois leather or a soft cloth moistened with a drop or two of vegetable oil. The final polish can be achieved in the same way using jewellers' rouge.

If a piece of jet needs dopping care is needed to prevent it from catching fire because it is a type of coal; cold dopping is therefore recommended. Jet can easily be faceted and the results are spectacular. Facets can be cut on sheets of fine abrasive paper laid on top of glass and then polished on very thin cloth or leather also laid over glass.

Amber

Amber is another organic material popular as jewellery and it has many of the same handling qualities as jet, being somewhat softer at $2\frac{1}{2}$ on Mohs' scale. Nevertheless, it is tough and will polish beautifully with jewellers' rouge on soft leather. However care must be taken not to rub too hard and generate excess frictional heat, because amber has a low melting point and the surface may fuse.

Amber is fossilized resin, and it comes in a range of colours and types, sometimes with perfectly preserved insects included, which were caught in the resin millions of years ago. Amber is found abundantly on the southern shores of the Baltic sea and as it floats in sea water pieces can sometimes be picked up on the beaches of East Anglia in England. One must be careful when buying amber, particularly finished goods, because it is so easily imitated by modern plastics, even to the extent of encapsulating insects. Genuine amber will float in a saturated solution of common salt, whereas most imitations sink. Lapidary magazines sometimes carry advertisements offering rough amber for sale.

Ivory

Turning from vegetable to animal matter there are two substances of interest to the carver: ivory and coral. Ivory may be taboo for many on account of the tragic massacre of elephants by ivory poachers, but it is still possible to pick up broken pieces of ivory in junk shops and it is superb material for carving. Its extreme toughness and fine grain have been exploited for centuries by carvers from the Far East who produced incredibly fine detail in their work. Ivory can be polished with finely powdered chalk (whiting) but it will deteriorate and crack if it becomes too dry. For this reason it should be kept away from radiators and bright lights.

Coral

Coral is no more difficult to work than shell, although it is usually to be had only in small pieces suitable for beads and little cabochons. It can stand up to intricate carving, rosebuds being a favourite theme. The most popular colour for branch coral is red, but it can be pink, white, orange or black as well.

Not so easily come by is fossilized coral. This is very beautiful material, but it is hard and calls for full lapidary treatment.

Fig. 50 Afro-Portuguese casket carved from ivory, probably sixteenth century, about 30 cm (12 in) high (courtesy Werner Forman Archive)

Fig. 51 Netsuke carved from ivory

Fig. 52 A coral pendant carved in the Orient

Fig. 53 Bowl, miniature vase and a bird carved from alabaster

Soft minerals

A few minerals with a hardness of 4 or less on Mohs' scale are well suited for carving by hand into small decorative pieces: animals, pin bowls, and miniature vases. Two of these minerals, rhodochrosite and malachite, are used extensively in jewellery, but they need to be protected by suitable mounting to prevent scratching. Here are some of the minerals suitable for hand work, in order of their hardness.

Talc

Talc, in the form of steatite, is commonly called soapstone because it has a greasy feeling. When polished it shines with a pearly lustre, and yet it is easily cut with a penknife.

Gypsum

Gypsum is easy to carve and polish in two of its varieties, the first being alabaster which can be bought in big pieces suitable for sculpture. The other variety, selenite or satin spar, is better for small carvings and it will polish to a very pretty satin lustre. Of course, finished articles from these very soft minerals are easily bruised and chipped.

Sepiolite

Sepiolite, better known as meerschaum, is not very common, but it is splendid material for carving. Tobacconists sell pipes carved from meerschaum, a favourite motif being a Turk's head.

Barytes

Barytes is a common material which takes on many different aspects. It is not difficult to pick up pieces of banded barytes in certain districts and this can be sliced and made into cabochons with steel tools.

Serpentine

Serpentine has always been a popular carving material and there still exists a thriving tradition in Cornwall for the benefit of visitors to The Lizard. Serpentine comes in a wide range of colour and grains and it handles well without splitting.

Aragonite

Aragonite, like barytes, can also be found in banded form and it is suitable for carving into cabochons.

Rhodochrosite and malachite

Rhodochrosite and malachite are the most attractive of the soft minerals and they are also the most expensive. Malachite is offered for sale by most dealers, but the supply of rhodochrosite and its prices vary considerably according to what is being mined in South Africa or South America where most of it comes from.

Without even using a hand wheel a beginner can carve pendants or cabochons from these showy stones which will come as a surprise to those who think that lapidary work is only for professionals with specialist equipment.

10 CARVING CABOCHONS

Cabochons are not as a rule carved, they are made on a grinding wheel. An interesting exercise and the next step in lapidary work is to carve a cabochon from one of the softer minerals; this can be done with the same materials and equipment already used for polishing pebbles and for flat lapping. An additional piece of gear which greatly simplifies handling is a bench hook.

Making a bench hook

If no proper bench is available work can be done on an ordinary table using a bench hook, which is a simple device with many uses for doing odd jobs. In this instance the bench hook is a double-decker. The dimensions given here are only an indication of size, and there is no need to keep to them if pieces of scrap wood are available. The whole thing can be made from 2 cm ($\frac{3}{4}$ in) chipboard, with a base measuring 15 × 15 cm (6 × 6 in). The first platform consists of two pieces 13 × 7 cm (5 × 3 in) glued one on top of the other with their ends flush to the left side of the base. The top deck is one piece 13 × 2.5 cm (5 × 1 in) glued with one edge flush to the back and one end to the left of the piece underneath. Another strip 15 × 5 cm (6 × 2 in) fixed underneath the front of the base forms the hook. Glue a piece of cloth onto the bottom to prevent damage to whatever the bench hook rests on.

Diag. 12 Double-decker bench hook

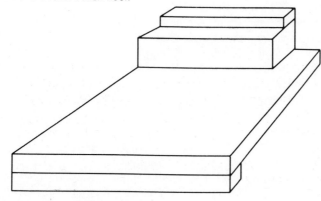

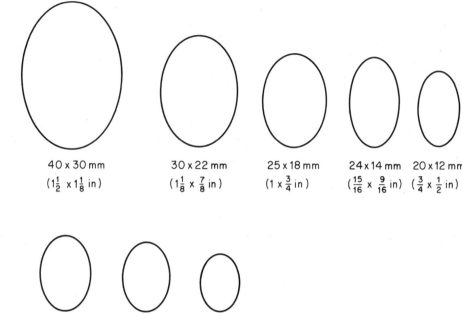

40 x 30 mm
$(1\frac{1}{2} \times 1\frac{1}{8}$ in)

30 x 22 mm
$(1\frac{1}{8} \times \frac{7}{8}$ in)

25 x 18 mm
$(1 \times \frac{3}{4}$ in)

24 x 14 mm
$(\frac{15}{16} \times \frac{9}{16}$ in)

20 x 12 mm
$(\frac{3}{4} \times \frac{1}{2}$ in)

20 x 15 mm
$(\frac{3}{4} \times \frac{5}{8}$ in)

18 x 13 mm
$(\frac{11}{16} \times \frac{1}{2}$ in)

15 x 12 mm
$(\frac{5}{8} \times \frac{1}{2}$ in)

Diag. 13 Templates for standard sizes of cabochons

Templates

Cabochons can be cut in many shapes—oval, circular, square, diamond—but as most of them are designed to be mounted as jewellery the most popular shape is an ellipse with a domed top. The top can be cut to a high or a shallow dome to suit the kind of stone being cut. Jewellery suppliers keep stocks of settings in base metal or silver to fit cabochons of standard sizes and lapidary suppliers have metal or plastic templates for drawing these sizes. If you know how to draw an ellipse you do not need a standard template and you can take maximum advantage of a piece of rough by not cutting away any more than necessary.

Having determined the maximum length and width of the biggest cabochon which can be cut from a piece of rough draw two lines aa and bb of this length on a piece of paper so that they intersect at right angles. Cut a narrow strip of stiff paper and draw a line across it near one end and make a small notch at each end of this line. From this line measure distance 'a' and distance 'b' and draw lines across the paper at these points marking the ends of the lines with arrowheads. If this strip of paper is now put over the intersecting lines 'aa' and 'bb' and rotated so that the two arrowheads are always just touching them, pencil dots made in the notch will produce a perfect ellipse when they are joined together.

Another method is to draw two circles and join them together with arcs.

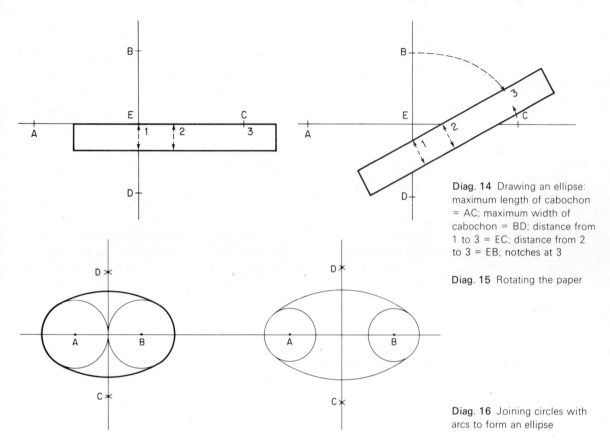

Diag. 14 Drawing an ellipse: maximum length of cabochon = AC; maximum width of cabochon = BD; distance from 1 to 3 = EC; distance from 2 to 3 = EB; notches at 3

Diag. 15 Rotating the paper

Diag. 16 Joining circles with arcs to form an ellipse

Making a cabochon

Before proceeding further it may be comforting to know that a man who had never before done any kind of lapidary work whatever made a 40 × 30 mm ($1\frac{1}{2}$ × $1\frac{1}{8}$ in) cabochon from a lump of rhodochrosite in less than two hours by this method, and this included the fifteen minutes needed to cut a slice from the lump of rough with an ordinary hacksaw. The only thing he did not do himself was to dop the stone when the time came. All the work was done on a bench hook on a kitchen table using only a hacksaw, file and flat silicon carbide grindstone, followed by sanding and polishing with the pebble polisher already described. Two hours may seem a long time to make a gem, but the latest polls in the United States prove that a man averages over three hours every day of the year watching television and a woman four hours.

The method described here is neither the quickest nor the easiest way to make cabochons; it is the way to do it without a workshop or any kind of machine—not even a bench grinder.

Rhodochrosite or malachite are two very good minerals for this project because they are both well-known gemstones, but they are relatively expensive and rhodochrosite is not over plentiful. Yet if you intend to put in two hours work to make a cabochon, it seems foolish to use a less attractive mineral merely to save a little money.

If rhodochrosite is chosen, it should be noted that this mineral has three distinct cleavage planes, and if it is roughly handled it may split along any one of them. In practice this means not using a coarse file or very rough grindstone for shaping, but fine ones. This stone is also heat sensitive and needs care when dopping, but wax can be used with moderate heat.

Malachite is brittle and chips easily; it is also poisonous and the dust from sawing and filing should not be inhaled. When working malachite by machine it is prudent to wear a mask, but in this instance, if plenty of water is used, the dust will not be troublesome. Powdered malachite is a soft green colour and it was used by Egyptian ladies 5,000 years ago for eye make-up.

When cutting a slice with a hacksaw the block of rough may need some support to keep it stable. It can be blocked up with dopwax to form a flat base, or it can be stuck to a piece of wood with waterglass. A piece of wood nailed to the right hand-side of the bench hook to act as a fence may also help. The thickness of the slice depends on the size of the finished cabochon and one measuring 40 × 30 mm ($1\frac{1}{2}$ × $1\frac{1}{8}$ in) needs to be about 8 mm ($\frac{5}{16}$ in) thick. Smaller cabochons will be thinner.

Having bought a slice, or cut one from the rough, the first thing is to examine it carefully on both sides and decide which is the better for the top; the losing side is then flat lapped on coarse grit to make a perfectly flat base. There is no need for further lapping on finer grit, nor need the top be lapped.

Fold a sheet of paper in half and cut a temporary template more or less to size, put this over the stone and turn it round until the best position is found. Getting this right makes all the difference between an interesting cabochon and a mediocre one. As a rule bands of colour look best running diagonally across a cabochon rather than straight up and down or across. There is no hard and fast rule, it is more a question of taste, and a little experimentation with a template will soon determine the best way to cut.

When this has been decided measure the length and breadth which can be fitted in and draw a template using these measurements. The ellipse so formed is now drawn on the base of the cabochon with an aluminium pencil. This is any thin piece of aluminium ground or filed to a point, and it is to be preferred to ball-point or felt-tipped pens because the ink sinks into soft stones and cannot be removed. Soft stones also absorb oil, and so a water-based lubricant is used when they are sawn on a machine.

Diag. 17 Finding the best position with a template

 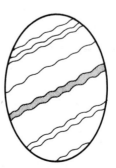 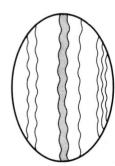

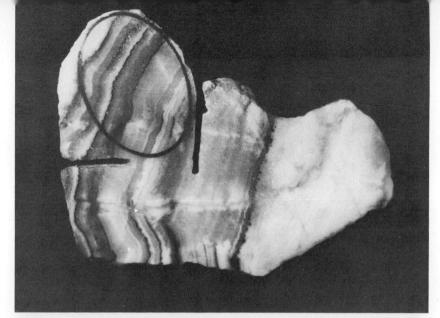

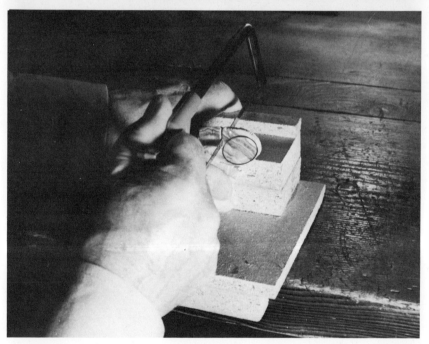

When it is clearly marked out, put the slab on the bench hook, with the outline uppermost, and with a small hacksaw, a medium file and a flat grindstone, trim it back to the outline. Stone can be nibbled away by gripping the edge with pincers or a Mole wrench, but this is a risky business and many a stone has been spoilt by doing it. It is only safe for very pronounced points which stick out. If things go wrong when nibbling, all that can be done is to make a smaller cabochon from the piece left. Use plenty of water to stop the tools from clogging up; this will make a mess, but it is assumed that the working surface has been covered with a sheet of waterproof plastic. A bowl of water should be near the work and the tools dried after use to prevent rust.

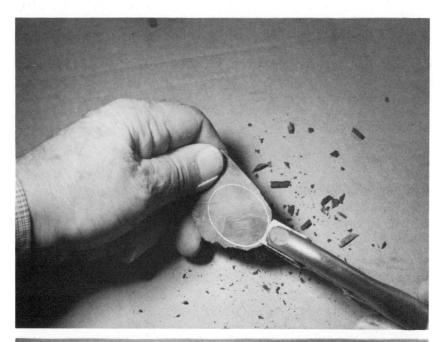

Fig. 57 Nibbling jasper with a Mole wrench

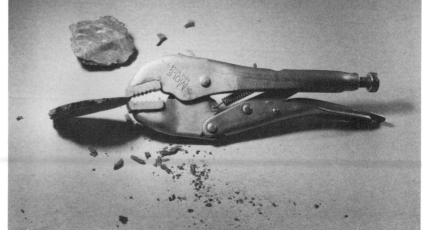

Fig. 58 Side view of the nibbling process

Fig. 59 The dopstick is held firmly on top of the bench hook when doming the stone

When all surplus material has been ground away the bottom edge of the blank is rubbed evenly all round on a sheet of medium grade abrasive paper to produce a slight chamfer; this is to prevent the edge from chipping. When this is done, draw with an aluminium pencil a line right round the edge about 1 mm ($\frac{1}{32}$ in) from the bottom to form a girdle. Doming is done down to this line and not below, leaving a narrow girdle instead of a sharp edge at the bottom.

The stone is now ready to be dopped on a straight dopstick by one of the methods already described. If the dopstick is put horizontally on the top deck of the bench hook it is easily held firm with the thumb of the left hand as the stone is domed. Doming is always done from the outside edge towards the middle, starting with a bevel at the sharp edge which is progressively brought down to the girdle and up towards the centre. This work can be done with a file or a grindstone, and the stone is turned round to keep a symmetrical shape when seen from the side or from the end. The most difficult part is to make an even dome without a flat spot in the middle.

When a good, regular dome has been achieved the file marks and any flat spots have to be sanded out and this is done with the pebble polisher. When a soft mineral is sanded with coarse paper it wears away rapidly, so while shaping the stone care must be taken to see that the doming is not brought down below the girdle. If this happens the stone will have a sharp edge which will chip and it will also be difficult to set it neatly in a bezel if it is mounted for jewellery.

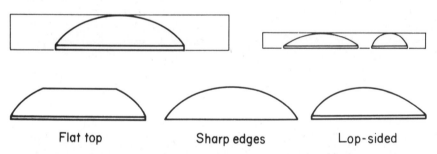

Diag. 18a High and low cabochons: a thick slice is required for a high dome or a big cabochon; only a shallow dome or a small cabochon can be cut from a thin slice

Flat top   Sharp edges   Lop-sided

Diag. 18b Common faults in doming cabochons

Fig. 60 Using the pebble polisher to sand a cabochon

83

Fig. 61 (Left) Finished cabochon in banded calcite – this material is difficult to polish without undercutting

Fig. 62 (Centre) Hand carved cabochon of sodalite mounted on a wooden napkin ring

Fig. 63 (Right) Maltese cross cut from a slice of Connemara marble with a hand carved cabochon of malachite in the centre

From this point sanding and polishing are carried out in exactly the same way as when polishing a pebble. Soft stones can be polished with Linde A on the leather lap. When the cabochon has no scratches on its surface and the best possible polish, take it off the dop and clean it thoroughly with detergent solution.

Cabochons made from hard stones

Small cabochons can be made from hard stones provided the original piece of rough does not require too much grinding. Shaping cannot be done with metal tools so the stone is first flat lapped to make a base and then lapped on the top until it is the right thickness. Sodalite, with a hardness of $5\frac{1}{2}$–6 is a very pretty stone rather like lapis lazuli, and it can be made into small cabochons suitable for a lady's ring without too much trouble. Labradorite and the variety called spectrolite are both 6–$6\frac{1}{2}$, and they have striking colour when the 'schiller' is oriented parallel to the base. Labradorite usually fractures into pieces which are easily cut into diamond shaped cabochons. These are original and striking gems, even though they are more difficult to fit into a setting.

There are a number of beaches in England and Scotland where pebbles of carnelian can be picked up. This beautiful, red variety of chalcedony is highly prized, and delightful cabochons can be ground by hand from small pebbles without undue effort. Polishing of these harder stones can be done with cerium oxide on the PVC lap using a length of cord to increase the speed.

Maltese Cross

A Maltese cross is not a cabochon, it is a trinket impossible to cut on a wheel but not at all difficult to make by hand in soft material. A square slice with a side of not less than 2.5 cm (1 in) will suffice and the thickness can be 6.5 mm ($\frac{1}{4}$ in). The cross must be designed so that the centre is left thick enough not to break easily. File and grind the slice to a

Fig. 64 Cutting out a Maltese cross with a hacksaw; the slice of Connemara marble has been backed with plastic to prevent breakages

perfect square, then flat lap and polish both sides and all four edges, making a very slight chamfer to prevent chipping.

Using waterglass, or some other water soluble glue, fix the square of stone to a strip of plywood the same width. This will make it easier to hold while the V shape notches are cut out with a fine hacksaw and will give added support to prevent breakage. Do not saw quite up to the lines but leave a margin for finishing. Sand the edges left by the saw with abrasive paper wrapped once round the blade of a straight table knife. Polish with a strip of leather glued to a very thin strip of wood or wrapped round a knife. Soak the stone and wood in water to separate them and finally chamfer any edges which have not yet been chamfered.

Nobody who has acquired a taste for lapidary work by making some of these things is likely to remain satisfied with this method of working for long. It is an excellent way of learning how to make cabochons, because the job is done in exactly the same sequence on a machine, but it is too slow to produce a satisfactory quantity for the amateur, and may result in discouragement. Without buying a machine, one can use a bench grinder for making cabochons even from agate and similar hard stones.

11 THE HAND WHEEL

The most efficient way to grind away surplus material is to use a fast moving, circular grindstone. The faster it turns the better it cuts, but safety limits have to be observed because grindstones can fly to pieces if they revolve too quickly. Machines sold for the use of amateurs usually have a 15 cm (6 in) diameter wheel provided with a metal guard and revolving at 1750 revolutions per minute. This speed is excellent for grinding and sanding, but it is too fast for polishing some minerals.

A grinding wheel cranked by hand may not reach a quarter of this speed, but nevertheless it will do good work, and it is a far more efficient method of working than those described so far. Such a wheel can be used to polish pebbles, to shape and polish cabochons from slices or small chunks of rough, even those with a hardness of 6 or more on Mohs' scale, and this covers all the quartzes, agates, chalcedony, jasper, flint etc. It can even be used for making small eggs and for pre-forming faceting material. A hand wheel is cheap, it can be carried about and set up on any firm surface, which makes it ideal for a caravan or holiday apartment. There is no need for a supply of power, and it makes very little noise. If a properly equipped workshop is out of the question this is the next best thing, and it even has one or two advantages, especially for polishing, because the speed is at all times under instant control.

The question may be asked, why bother with a hand wheel, why not use an electric drill? There are several good reasons for not using a drill, the first and most important being that lapidary work needs to be done with plenty of water and most electric drills run off mains electricity of 220 volts alternating current. The combination of wet hands and mains electricity is extremely dangerous and can be lethal. Secondly, an electric drill is too fast for lapidary work and it is not the right thing for a 15 cm (6 in) grinding wheel. Canvas buffs can be used for some types of polishing, but it is not wise to try working stones with an electric drill.

To set up a hand wheel, the first thing is to buy a bench grinder. Not every tool shop stocks them because they are not so much in demand as they were, but they are still being made for sharpening tools. Choose one with a 12 mm ($\frac{1}{2}$ in) arbor to take a 15 cm (6 in) silicon carbide grindstone of 2.5 cm (1 in) thickness. The grinder will already be fitted with a grindstone, but it is unlikely to be the right kind for lapidary work. The correct grindstones can be bought from a rock shop rather than a tool shop. The gearing should give a multiplication of 9 or 10, which means that the wheel goes round nine times for every turn of the handle. Before buying, test the grinder for noise, because some models have gears inside which whine at top speed.

The following accessories can be bought from a rock shop: one silicon carbide 15 cm (6 in) wheel 2.5 cm (1 in) wide, 100 grit; a second similar wheel of 220 grit (useful but not essential); silicon carbide wet/dry sanding discs of the same diameter in grades 100, 300 and 500, or nearest (you can cut your own discs from rectangular sheets of paper and save money); one disc of thick rubber the same size, and one felt and one leather disc for polishing. This completes the list of things to be bought with the exception of a few pieces of wood for making a mount and a large G clamp for fixing the grinder to a table, if it is not already fitted with one. The total cost of all this can be ascertained beforehand but it should not be very much. Bear in mind that if at some later date you buy a machine, all the grinding wheels, sanding discs and polishing laps will fit on a machine. The bench grinder will still be extremely useful for polishing and, perhaps, for taking on holiday.

Although it can be clamped just as it comes, on a table, it is worth while taking the trouble to mount it on a small platform with splash-guard and water supply. In the long run this makes for easier working and saves time. As there will be a good deal of water flying around, make a base from plastic-covered chipboard, or from wood and paint it.

The dimensions of the one in the illustration are given here, but this is only an indication, as bench grinders come in different sizes. The base is made from chipboard 2 cm ($\frac{3}{4}$ in) thick and measures 30 × 20 cm (12 × 8 in). The platform needs to be high enough to give room for one's knuckles underneath the handle at its lowest point, so that the grinder can be fixed anywhere along the bench, not just at the end. Fix the grinder with long screws going down into the upright piece supporting the platform.

The splash-guard in the illustration consists of a strip of aluminium 3 mm ($\frac{1}{8}$ in) thick and 5 cm (2 in) wide. The advantage of aluminium is that it can easily be bent and is no harder than wood for cutting and drilling. Screw the splash-guard to the platform and it can support a drip water supply of absurd simplicity. With a hot needle pierce a tiny hole in the bottom of a plastic container (a yoghourt pot) and fix it above a strip of absorbent material long enough to reach the wheel. There are squares of absorbent tissue sold for washing up, which do splendidly. The pot is fixed to a piece of metal with adhesive tape and secured in place with a clip of some sort; a clothes peg will do. Water is poured into the pot as required and is fed to the wheel to prevent clogging. Professional lapidaries in the famous centre of Idar Oberstein in West Germany use a drip system like this and some of them use folded newspaper as the absorbent material.

The outfit needs a sump at the bottom to collect the water, and this can be made from a plastic bottle cut in half. If the bottle is too narrow it can be opened out by heating it in boiling water, or near a flame when it will become soft and pliable. Attach this sump to the splash-guard so that it can be emptied occasionally.

Fig. 65 Bench grinder fitted with a lapidary's grindstone, drip feed, splash-guard and pan, mounted on a shelf; note the use of the hand rest for the one hand which is working

Fig. 66 Sanding disc attached to a rubber pad, which in turn is fixed to a small grindstone unsuitable for lapidary use

Fig. 67 Making a drum sander from a grindstone

The whole unit can be firmly clamped to any table with a big G clamp, but this may not be good for the table. An alternative is to fix a strip of wood underneath the front of the base to make a bench hook, then tie a cord to the back of the platform, bring it round underneath the table, pull tight, and fix it to the front of the base.

A hand wheel can be used in three ways, first grinding on the rim of a wheel, then sanding and polishing on flat discs, and lastly sanding and polishing on a drum.

Flat discs need to be supported on a pad of soft rubber which will give slightly under pressure from the stone. These can be bought, or cut from the sort of rubber used to make diving suits. Sponge plastic is not resilient enough and tears away too easily. If the grinder was sold with a wheel not suitable for lapidary work this will be ideal if the rubber pad is glued to it.

Otherwise use a wooden disc or a discarded saw blade. Sanding discs and polishing laps are fixed to the rubber pad with 'on/off cement' and there is no need to unscrew the nut every time they are changed. It is a good thing if the rubber pad is a little larger than the support underneath, but not larger than the discs.

A drum sander is useful but not essential, although some jobs cannot be done without one. The same stone used for the flat discs can be used if the rim is covered with soft rubber; otherwise a drum must be made from wooden discs with a rim not less than 2.5 cm (1 in) wide. Cover the circumference with soft rubber or moquette with the pile underneath and then bind all round with a strip of the adhesive plastic tape used for packing parcels. The shiny side of this tape makes a very good base for a coating of 'on/off cement' to hold strips of sanding paper or felt or leather for polishing. There will be a join in the sanding paper because the rectangular sheets are not big enough to cut a long enough strip.

A useful accessory, soon made from scrap, is a jig for resting dopsticks on when making circular cabochons or pre-forms for faceting. It consists quite simply of a piece of chipboard fixed on edge to another piece which is the base. The base rests on the platform and is held in place with a small G clamp, and a notch is cut from the corner of the upright piece at such a height that when a dopstick is held in the notch the stone is at the correct height for grinding against the rim of the wheel. Dimensions will vary with the size of the grinder, but the one shown here was made from one piece of chipboard 15 × 12 × 2 cm (6 × 4½ × ¾ in) on a base 15 × 7.5 × 1 cm (6 × 3 × ½ in).

Fig. 68 Sanding a concave surface on a drum sander

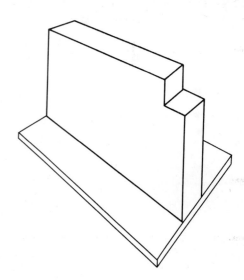

Diag. **19** Jig for circular cabochons and pre-forms

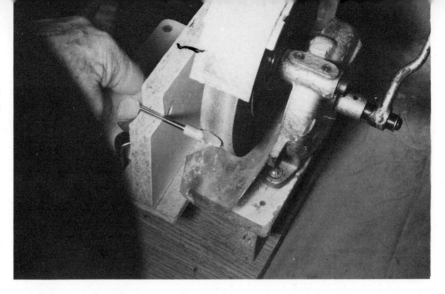

Fig. 69 Using the jig to pre-form a piece of quartz for faceting

When a circular cabochon is to be made the jig is clamped parallel to the face of the wheel to make a circular blank, and then it is turned at an angle as the stone is bevelled. In this way a cone-shaped pre-form can be made for a standard brilliant when faceting.

Making an oval cabochon

Cabochons can be made on a hand wheel in exactly the same way as on a machine but there are two differences. The wheel does not revolve so fast and the lapidary will have to hold the stone with one hand unless somebody else can be persuaded to turn the handle. The effect of slower speed is that the grinding will take longer and the grindstone wears out more quickly. It is much harder for someone without experience to work with one hand and this is why it is advisable to work with other people at a club or school, or persuade a friend to join in. Two people can work together each having a spell on turning the handle.

Before going any further it is only fair to point out that making cabochons is bad for fingernails on both hand wheels and machines. In the early stage the stone blank is not put on a dop until it has been ground to shape, it is held between finger and thumb. It is very easy indeed to grind notches in the nail of the index finger, and although this may not trouble males it could provide sufficient justification for a girl to decide that making cabochons is not for her. This does not mean that she has to abandon lapidary work, on the contrary, there is every reason to believe that girls excel at the fine, detailed manipulation needed for faceting.

For a first attempt at using a wheel it will be more interesting to tackle material which is too hard to be easily shaped otherwise. Many beautiful kinds of agate can now be bought ready sliced, or one may find a piece of rough small enough not to need trimming on a saw. If rough is used, begin by grinding a more or less flat base on the edge of the wheel and then lap it quite flat on a sheet of glass. It is not good practice to use the face of a wheel to try to grind a flat surface.

Hold the stone between finger and thumb against the edge of the wheel just below its widest point. Keep a steady drip of water and dip the stone in a bowl of water from time to time. Working wet does three things, it keeps down dust, it keeps the stone clean and prevents the wheel from clogging, and it prevents unwanted heat build-up. If the stone is held in one place and not moved from side to side across the working surface of the wheel it will soon wear a groove in the wheel. This is almost bound to happen, but an effort must be made to keep it to a minimum as a true wheel is needed for accurate work.

When a perfectly flat surface has been prepared for the base of the cabochon, the shape is drawn on it with an aluminium pencil. Grind away surplus material until the blank conforms to the outline drawn on the base, and then to prevent the lower edge of the base from chipping, rub it all round on a piece of medium grade paper to form a slight chamfer.

The stone is next ground to a dome, and as has already been explained the height of the dome depends on the size of the cabochon and also on any special optical characteristics of the material in use. Assuming that a medium curvature is aimed at, for a first attempt, begin by holding the stone—still not dopped—with the base upwards and grind a bevel all round leaving a narrow girdle at the bottom. Doming is always done from the outside towards the centre, and not the other way round. Keep rotating the stone as the dome progresses and hold it up to the light occasionally to make sure that the slope is even and the silhouette is symmetrical when seen both from the side and the end. If the stone is a small one it may need dopping to do this properly, but in any case, as soon as a good shape has been achieved, without a flat spot at the top, the stone has to be dopped for sanding.

Working a dopped stone against the wheel or on a sanding disc calls for a special technique which is more easily acquired by using two hands. One hand holds the stick close behind the stone and the other one rotates the stick at the other end. Once the movement has been mastered, and it is not difficult, then it can be done with one hand. Its purpose is to keep the stone constantly moving so that a smooth surface is created free from flat spots. If a finer grindstone of 220 grit is available, the stone can be smoothed on this before sanding first on coarse paper then on medium and fine. Washing stone and hands is necessary at each stage to avoid contamination, and the stone should be dried and examined through a magnifying glass to make sure there are no scratches made by coarser grit than the one being used.

If any difficulty is experienced in forming a good, regular surface, you can use the frame for polishing pebbles. This gives a very good shape to a cabochon particularly where the dome meets the girdle. The most important part of polishing any stone is the final preparation before polishing. When in doubt about whether the stone is ready to polish, continue sanding a little longer on fine paper because any blemishes which are not completely removed will show up when the surface is polished. When this happens there is no alternative to going back to a previous stage and repeating the sanding process unless you are prepared to keep a permanent monument to sloppy workmanship.

Replace the fine sanding disc with the appropriate polishing lap, taking

Fig. 70 Polishing on a felt pad

great care not to get silicon carbide on the lap. The lap should be sprayed to keep it moist, and a very little polishing powder spread over it. The handle is turned gently and the stone applied to the lap with slight pressure to avoid building up too much heat. At the same time move the stone all the time so that no one spot can be overheated. Stones will crack or discolour when overheated at the polishing stage, and this is very disappointing. Polish comes up quite quickly if the right combination of polish and lap has been chosen, and the time when it appears is usually just as the lap begins to dry out. It must not be allowed to dry completely because dry polish scratches instead of polishing. Make quite sure that all the sides are polished down to the girdle; it is easy to miss patches. When satisfied that a good polish has been achieved all over, take the stone off the dop and clean it thoroughly.

At a later stage one should look into the possibility of using diamond compound for sanding and polishing even though one cannot afford diamond grinding wheels. They can be used on a hand wheel or a machine and the technique is the same as for grit. The work is done more quickly and with less mess, but the initial cost is considerably more than for grit. In the long run some workers maintain that diamond actually does not cost any more. There is plenty of time to decide on priorities as the beginner gains more skill, but the option of using diamond should not be forgotten. Some of the diamond compound used for polishing cabochons can also be used for faceting.

All kinds of cabochons can be made on a hand wheel, the only limit being the amount of grinding needed to produce intricate shapes. When you have made several straightforward oval cabochons by this method it is time to experiment with different shapes and materials and combinations of both. Among the possibilities are: double-sided cabochons in the shape of a heart, a pear, a cross or a tusk; standard cabochons from translucent stones; small eggs and beads. A great deal depends on the shape of the original piece of rough and whether there is a chance of using a trim saw to prepare it before grinding. The astute amateur will go through a dealer's stock and pick out those pieces which need a minimum of grinding.

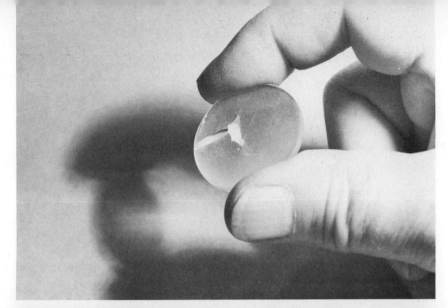

Fig. 71 A quartz disc cracked by overheating on a felt lap when polishing

Fig. 72 Heart and pear shaped cabochons and a small egg, all made from beach pebbles

Heart-shaped pendant

This can be made from a slice or even from a flat pebble. When drawing the outline of the heart, make the notch at the top very wide so that the angle is more than 90° and can be cut on the corner of the wheel. When the stone has been ground to the outline, draw a line all round the edge midway between the two faces and dome each side to this line, but do not make too sharp an edge. Do not attempt more than slight doming at the top where the notch is, otherwise there will be difficulty in shaping the cleavage. This shape is easier to sand and polish on a drum rather than a flat disc. If a small hole is wanted for mounting, it can be drilled by hand using a 1.5 mm ($\frac{1}{16}$ in) diamond drill.

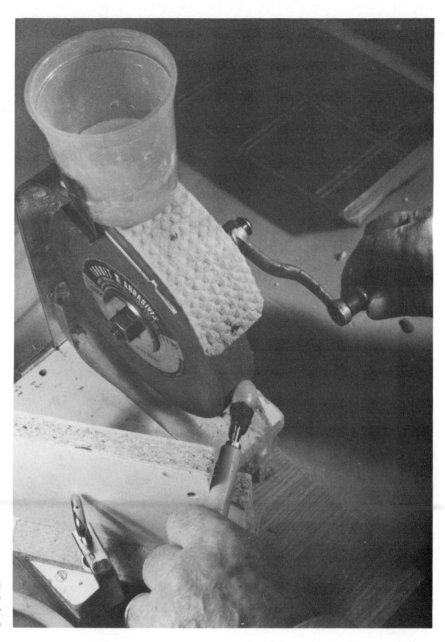

Fig. 73 Making a small egg out of quartz showing how the jig can be clamped at any desired angle

Pear-shaped pendant

If the piece of rough lends itself to this, a pear-shaped pendant can be made either with a flat back or rounded on both faces. The point has to be quite blunt otherwise it is almost certain to break off.

Clear quartz with inclusions of rutile or tourmaline makes beautiful double-sided cabochons because some light is reflected from the back and enhances the appearance of the needles inside. The back can be flat or domed.

Cross

Crosses can be cut from hard material on a grinding wheel if the wheel is kept true and a design chosen which does not demand too much grinding. Crosses can be flat both sides, domed in front and flat at the back, or domed either side. Doming should only be attempted over the whole surface of the stone and can best be done before the arms are ground to shape. Trying to dome each separate arm will be troublesome.

The arms are ground out on the edge of the wheel which must be quite true and not grooved. If the wheel is grooved it must be dressed. There are special tools for dressing wheels, but the job can be done by holding a thick iron bolt across the cutting edge of the wheel and grinding into it until the groove has disappeared. When grinding the arms of a cross remember the curvature of the wheel and allow a slight margin to be finished by hand with a flat piece of grindstone. Sanding and polishing will be easier on a drum but it is possible to work on the edge of a flat disc. All sharp edges should be given a very slight chamfer to minimise chipping.

Egg

It is quite possible to make small eggs, the size of blackbirds' eggs without any more apparatus than the jig suggested for circular cabochons. First rough out the shape of the egg freehand, holding the stone in the fingers, then carefully dop it at one end making certain it is centred and straight on the dop. Using the jig, grind the widest part to a true circle, and then by gradually altering the angle of the jig, grind the egg to its narrower end. Take it off the dop and reverse it and then grind the thick end. Sand and polish this end, then reverse dop once more and complete.

Flat-ended pillow

A very neat cabochon shaped like a pillow with sloping, faceted ends can be made partly on the wheel and partly on a flat lap. The basic shape is half a cylinder, so begin by grinding a rectangular base about three times as long as it is wide and then dop it carefully on the dopstick used for random faceting. Grind the top to make a half cylinder, but it can with advantage be somewhat hog-backed. Grind the two ends to a flat surface sloping inwards ready for flat lapping, and then sand and polish the curved part. Take the stone to the flat lap and grind and polish the end facets using the gadget for random faceting.

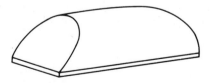

Diag. 20 Pillow-shaped cabochon with faceted ends

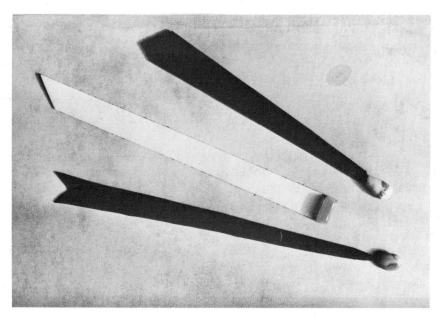

Fig. 74 Bookmarkers made from cabochons and thin leather

Bookmarkers

If one of the above shaped cabochons is glued across a strip of fine, gloving leather it makes a most acceptable bookmarker. The leather should be measured to lie the length of the book—which may be 25 cm (10 in)—plus 5 cm (2 in) to allow a short extension beyond the head and foot of the closed book. The leather should also be cut with a sharp craft knife and straight-edge, rather than with scissors, to give a perfect edge.

Translucent cabochons

Cabochons cut from opaque minerals rely for their effect on colouring and shape, but translucent stones are very beautiful if they are properly cut to display the effect of light reflected from inside the stone. Moonstone with its characteristic blue flash is a good example, and there is nothing to stop a beginner from cutting a small cabochon from moonstone on a hand wheel once he knows how it is done. The trick is to understand how to orient the material correctly, and this means cutting the base in the correct plane in relation to the way the light is reflected from inside the stone.

Orienting moonstone

Moonstone is a feldspar of hardness 6–6½, and the best quality reflects a flash of blue light when held in a certain position. This mineral has distinct cleavage, and breaks easily if roughly handled, and nearly all the cabochons on sale are very small. Sometimes lapidaries from Asian countries try to make the most of their precious material and do not orient the stones properly so that the blue flash appears at one end of the stone instead of in the centre.

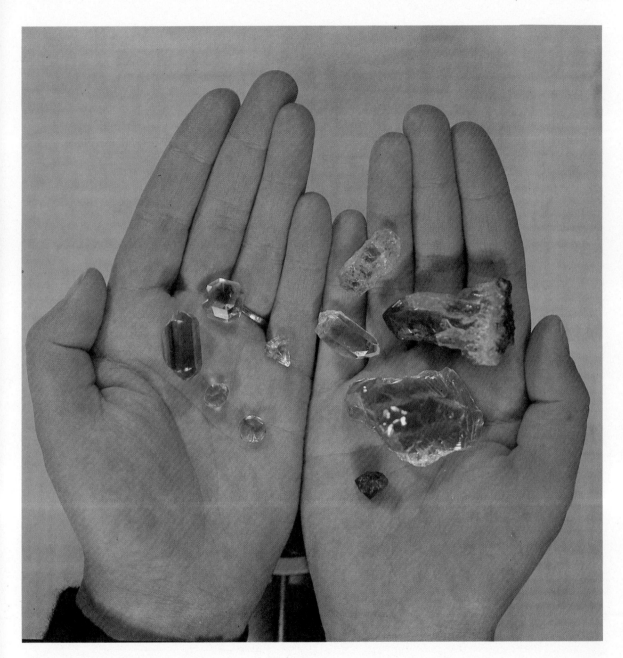

Roughs and hand faceted stones

Faceted stones: (top) cut corner kite in aquamarine, standard round brilliant in amethyst, (centre) standard round brilliant in clear quartz, rectangular step cut in smoky quartz, (bottom) standard round brilliant in amethyst, cut corner square with pyramid pavilion in amethyst

Take a piece of moonstone in your hands and stand directly under an unshaded electric light bulb, looking down at the stone, which should be just clear of the shadow of your forehead. Turn the stone in all directions until you can see a yellowish, satin sheen which is not the reflection of the electric light from the surface but which seems to be inside the stone. Keeping the stone so that the sheen is in a horizontal plane rest it on a lump of plasticine and draw a pencil line all round with a pencil supported on something the right height. If this has been done properly, the stone can be turned upside down and the sheen will appear in the same plane on the opposite side. If a cabochon is cut with its base in this plane it will have a yellowish gleam of light when polished; but a much more attractive blue flash will result if the stone is cut at right angles to this plane.

Still under the light bulb, hold the stone with the pencil mark in a vertical plane all the time. Sooner or later, a fainter sheen, rather more blue than the first one, will be noticed. To make quite certain, turn the stone upside down and the blue sheen should re-appear on the other side. Once more, hold the stone in the position where this blue sheen is horizontal and mark another girdle round the stone. The stone has now been correctly oriented and any cabochon cut with its base parallel to the second girdle will have a blue flash when finished.

Start by grinding a flat base and then check that it is in the correct position by rotating the stone horizontally through 360°. The sheen should remain visible all the time, and if it is not, the base must be re-ground at the right inclination. Once this is right the rest of the work is quite straightforward, and the best effect comes from an oval or circular cabochon with a pronounced high dome. A further check can be made when the dome is being ground, as it is most irritating to have a finished gem with a flash which keeps veering off to one side. If the flash is not in the right place, go back and re-grind the base and then the top of the stone. In moonstone the flash seems to float over the surface after the final polish.

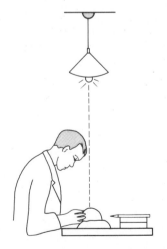

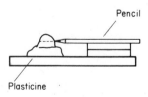

Pencil

Plasticine

Diag. 21 Orienting moonstone

Labradorite

Two other feldspars, labradorite and its cousin spectrolite, are much easier to deal with. When held in a certain position these minerals display a flash of brilliant colour known as a 'schiller', and it can be blue, green, gold or a mixture of colours. Using the same procedure under an electric light it is easy to determine the plane of the schiller and then cut a base parallel to it. However, to make the most of it the cabochon should be cut with a shallow dome and not a high one.

Cat's-eye stones

There are a few minerals which can be cut to make a cat's-eye effect. This results from a series of parallel fibres running through the stone and the cat's-eye can only be cut properly if the rough has been sliced exactly parallel to these fibers. Tiger-eye agate is fairly plentiful and not expensive, but when buying slices make quite sure that they have been cut correctly. This material has honey coloured bands alternating with brown ones, and when the stone is looked at from the opposite side the bands change colour and are seen in reverse.

Conventional cabochons in tiger-eye agate are oriented so that the fibres run squarely across the stone parallel to the short axis of the oval. When cut with a fairly high dome the effect will be a narrow band of light moving parallel to the long axis.

These are some of the things which can be done with a hand wheel, and it is assumed that while acquiring skill in handling gemstones the beginner will also have amassed a useful store of information from books on minerals and lapidary techniques which treat these subjects in greater detail.

12 CHOOSING RAW MATERIAL

The choice of materials suitable for working by hand is bound to be limited if they cannot be sawn to a convenient size. The problem is largely solved now that rock shops are offering a good selection of minerals ready sliced for making cabochons. Surplus material has to be removed by grinding, but there is another way, and that is to 'nibble' from the edge of the slice. This method can be used effectively with soft stones and with some of the harder ones too, if one is prepared to take the risk of an unfortunate break now and again.

Hold the slice of rock in one hand and with a large pair of pincers, or better still, a Mole wrench, take a grip on the very edge and squeeze hard. If a small piece does not crumble away under pressure then press down until it breaks off. The process is continued until the slice is trimmed roughly to the shape required, but it is risky to go too near the final outline because one does not have enough control over the pieces which break away. It is better to leave a good margin to be ground away rather than to finish up with a small stone because of an unfortunate break. Serpentines and marbles respond well to this treatment, but minerals with cleavage planes are tricky. Even harder minerals can be 'nibbled' if the slices are not too thick, one example being turritella agate.

Fig. 75 Turritella agate showing the remains of shells

99

Fig. 76 Trimming rough rock
with a hammer

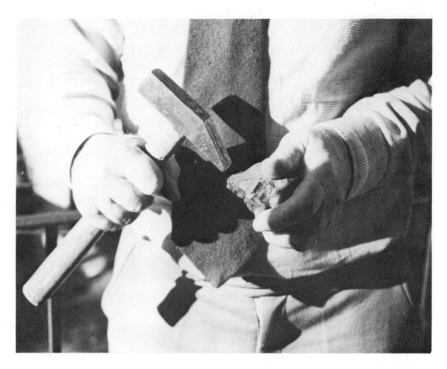

Large pieces of rough can be trimmed with a hammer, which is useful for some of the pieces collected on field trips. The technique is to hold the rock in your left hand—having removed any wrist watch—and grip the hammer in the right hand very close to the head. Using the wrist as a fulcrum, with short sharp jabs, move the hammer head through the arc of a circle so that it only just makes contact with the edge of the rock. After a few blows in the same place, pieces of rock will flake off, and these may be of the right size for making cabochons. When doing this it is essential to wear goggles or an eye shield as a protection against splinters. Breaking down rocks with a hammer and cold chisel is a somewhat wasteful process, not recommended for valuable material. Note that ordinary carpenter's hammers are not the right kind for this work; you should have a mason's or a geological hammer; the ones sold for schools are quite adequate.

Many pebbles are so shaped that very little grinding is needed to make them into symmetrical cabochons, and these are excellent material for hand workers. It may even be possible to arrange with friends or pen-friends to pick up material when they go on holiday, provided they can be relied on to know what is worth while picking up. A hand worker soon becomes very conscious of what is worth spending time and effort on, and for this reason it is sound policy always to buy the finest quality one can afford.

There is less difficulty in choosing material for faceting by hand. Faceting grade minerals are expensive and part of the art of the faceter is to make the largest gem possible from any given piece of rough. This means that a minimum of material has to be ground away. Some dealers offer pre-forms, that is pieces which have been roughly shaped and need no further grinding or sawing before being faceted. If a faceter can join a club and have access to a machine occasionally then it will not take long to prepare several pre-forms for faceting at home.

A very simple way to find inexpensive faceting material, especially when learning, is to look through the piles of tumbled stones which are sold at so much each. It is easy to pick out pieces which are free from flaws and which have the best colour, and the average selection will include amethyst, smoky quartz, citrine and sometimes very small pieces of aquamarine. All these are good for hand faceting.

Returning to cabochons, there are quite a number of minerals of low and medium hardness which will look well as cabochons, the two most striking being rhodochrosite and malachite, which have already been mentioned, but good colour and marking can be found in marbles, serpentines and banded calcite. As a general rule the brightest and most durable cabochons will be made from minerals of hardness above 5 on Mohs' scale. Here is a list of minerals which can be turned into cabochons by a hand worker, with some notes on the best way to handle them.

Serpentine (H $2\frac{1}{2}$–4)

So called because the green variety is reminiscent of a serpent's skin with fine green and black mottling. Cornish serpentine can also be a deep red flecked with different colours. Verdite and bowenite are names to describe serpentine from overseas countries. This relatively soft material is apt to absorb oil and should not be marked with a felt pen. Work it with plenty of water for grinding and sanding. It will not take a mirror finish when polished but a pleasant lustrous sheen. The best way to polish without undercutting is to use Linde A on a leather lap at slow speed. The attractive yellow and green marble from Connemara can be treated in the same way.

Malachite (H 3–4)

This striking, bright green mineral with contrasting bands of colour is occasionally chatoyant. In spite of being rather brittle it can be shaped into cabochons without difficulty, using plenty of water to keep down the dust which is toxic and should not be inhaled or swallowed. Do not lick malachite to moisten it. Polishing is not easy; the recommended procedure is to use a very wet slurry of chrome oxide on a leather buff, and this gives good results. However chrome oxide is extremely messy and it stains everything bright green. Cleaning up can best be done with a hand cleaner (such as 'Swarfeega') following the makers' instructions, but if chrome oxide is used on stones which are not green it will be almost impossible to dislodge it from any crevices. The alternative is to use Linde A which will give a good polish on a leather lap. Malachite, like rhodochrosite and the serpentines, is absorbent and when sawn oil should not be used as a lubricant.

Rhodochrosite (H 3–4)

This is another strikingly beautiful mineral, raspberry pink with whitish bands. It splits easily along cleavage planes and is heat sensitive, so accidents can be expected. Nevertheless it can be made into cabochons on a hand wheel, preferably using a 220 grinding wheel rather than a 100 wheel, and plenty of water all the time when grinding and sanding. Use Linde A on leather for polishing and a cold method for dopping.

Lapis lazuli (H $5\frac{1}{2}$)

This is a beautiful, traditional gemstone consisting of three different minerals each of a different hardness, which makes polishing difficult. The finest deep blue lapis comes from Afghanistan and a lighter colour comes from Chile. It wears away grindstones quickly and should be ground with plenty of water. Unless the stone is of very high quality it is bound to have a few whitish patches in it and these tend to undercut. Golden flecks of pyrites add to the attraction of the stone and do not present any difficulty. To avoid undercutting, sand very wet with light pressure and polish at low speed with Linde A on leather. In any case, lapis lazuli does not take a very high polish, as you may see by looking in almost any jeweller's window.

Sodalite (H $5\frac{1}{2}$)

Very suitable material for amateurs, sodalite is deep blue resembling the blue part of lapis. It is cheap, is not sensitive to heat and presents no difficulty apart from a tendency to chip round the edges. A good polish can be had with cerium oxide on a leather lap. This is excellent material for making cabochons on a hand wheel because it is not too hard and the finished gem has a most professional look about it.

Feldspar (H 6–$6\frac{1}{2}$)

Amazonite, moonstone, sunstone, labradorite and spectrolite are included in this mineral group and they are stones of remarkable beauty when properly treated. They are translucent and owe their popularity to the optical effects revealed by skilful cutting. The best quality moonstone shows a blue flash, and the next best a silver one. There is a special word 'adularescence' used to describe the sheen displayed by these stones, which is hard to describe.

Labradorite and spectrolite have a different kind of sheen which is called a 'schiller'. The difference between these two can only be appreciated by looking at finished stones. The way to orient stones with these special optical characteristics has been described in detail in the previous chapter. Feldspars are not as hard as the quartz family, but unlike them they have cleavage planes and tend to split along them with rough treatment, however they are insensitive to heat and can be dopped with wax. An excellent polish can be produced with cerium oxide on a felt lap.

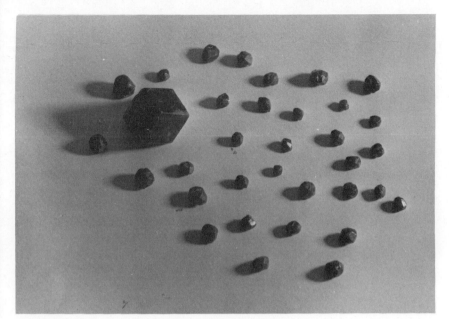

Fig. 77 Almandine garnet

Garnets (H $6\frac{1}{2}$–$7\frac{1}{2}$)

Garnets are divided into six different groups and they come in a whole range of colours. The rarest and most expensive is a superb emerald green called demantoid garnet, but this is top class gem material outside the scope of the beginner. Deep red almandine garnet is plentiful and reasonable in price. Small pieces can be turned into cabochons on a hand wheel, but this material on account of its lack of cleavage and its high refractive index is ideal for faceting by hand. The high refractive index means that, if the critical angles are respected, garnet will flash more brightly than quartz when the gem is faceted. The only drawback is a certain brittleness which demands careful grinding. Polish cabochons of garnet with Linde A on leather, and facets with cerium oxide on PVC sheet.

Flint (H $6\frac{1}{2}$)

Flint is a form of opaque chalcedony which is very much neglected in lapidary books, yet in some areas it is plentiful and can be had in many different colours—red, yellow, grey, black and white. Sometimes it is banded and sometimes it can be cut to show 'pictures'. The South Downs are covered with flint concretions, which are nodules of flint many of which have formed round fossil sponges. When these are sawn in half and polished on a flat lap they become collectors' items. Some of them have crystals in the centre and occasionally broken ones can be picked up which can be ground and polished without the need for a saw. Pebbles of flint can be given a brilliant polish once the outside crust has been ground off and they are some of the most interesting and attractive pebbles one can have. The beaches of Brighton or Dieppe will provide enough to keep a hand worker busy for a lifetime. Flint is polished in the same way as agate.

Fig. 78 Flint concretions: the large one with the fossilized sponge came from the ballast of an abandoned railway line, the three hollow hemispheres from a cemetery

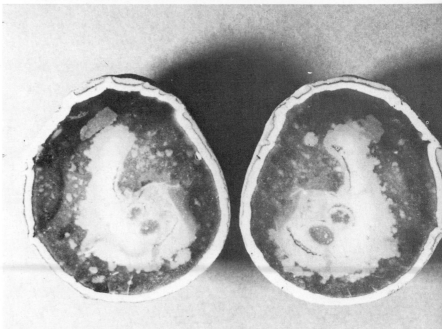

Fig. 79 Flint concretions from the South Downs, when sawn in half, hand lapped and polished, become collector's pieces

Quartz (H 7)

Quartz in its various forms is cheap and plentiful and there is nothing better for learning to facet. Rose quartz looks very pretty in large lumps but is disappointingly pale in pieces of cabochon size. It is also very prone to be full of fractures. Smoky quartz makes such beautiful gems that it is often, deceitfully, passed off as topaz. Citrine is yellow and amethyst is purple quartz, and rock crystal is the term used to describe quartz which is as clear as ice. Quartz having no cleavage planes and being heat resistant is straightforward material for all lapidary work and takes a high polish with cerium or tin oxide on felt for cabochons and PVC for facets. Particularly attractive is quartz containing golden needles of rutile or black ones of tourmaline.

Crysocolla is a bright, peacock-green form of quartz which comes on the market at irregular intervals, so an opportunity to acquire a piece at a reasonable price should not be missed. It does chip easily at the edges and it must be polished with care because if it gets too hot white spots appear. Nevertheless it is superb material for making pendants and cabochons of unusual appearance.

Agates (H 7)

Agates include chalcedony, jasper and onyx. There is a bewildering choice available, including lace agate, moss agate, tiger-eye, fossilized wood etc; whole books have been written about agates. All of them are about the same hardness and they nearly all polish to a mirror finish. The

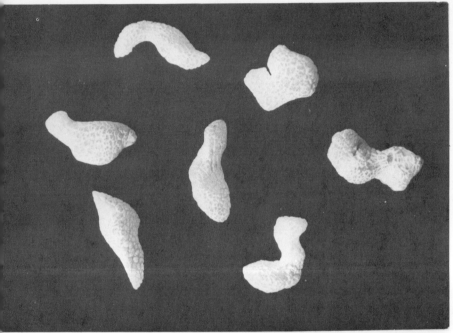

Fig. 80 Snake skin agates from the United States

Fig. 81 Fossilized wood from Scotland

Fig. 82 Agates from Brazil, South Africa, India, Botswana and Queensland

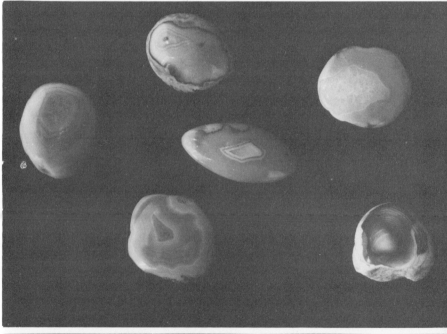

Fig. 83 Pink agates from Botswana, none longer than 2 cm ($\frac{3}{4}$ in)

Fig. 84 Small pieces of tourmaline suitable for hand work

hand worker is at a disadvantage because of their hardness, but small pieces do exist which can be worked without sawing. Exceptionally pretty and small enough to be tackled by hand are the pink Botswana agates; even broken pieces can be turned into delightful cabochons. Not quite so colourful but also small are the pebble agates from Queensland, Australia, which have a rough outside. They are rather more troublesome than Botswana agates because they are often flawed and this cannot be seen until they have been ground smooth. All the other agates can be worked on a hand wheel if trimmed slices can be had of the right size. Polishing is done with cerium or tin oxide on felt. Flat surfaces on PVC sheet.

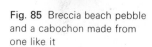

Tourmaline (H 7–7$\frac{1}{2}$)

Tourmaline forms in long prisms of triangular cross section often with rounded faces. The colour range is extensive, green being the best known, but also red, black, brown blue and pink. Sometimes the colour of a single crystal changes along its length or from the centre to the outside, as in 'water melon' tourmaline where the centre is pink and the outside green. In spite of its brittleness, tourmaline is good material for the amateur for both cabochons and faceting. It is strongly dichroic and on account of this it is usually faceted in a step cut in the direction of the axis of the crystal parallel to its length. When cut across its length the colour is usually too dark. The main drawback about tourmaline is that it is often a mass of fractures, so it is wise to buy good quality rough.

Fig. 85 Breccia beach pebble and a cabochon made from one like it

Miscellaneous

All the minerals listed above are conventional grist for the lapidary's mill, but one of the joys of this hobby is finding unusual pieces of rock, stone, shell or pebble for oneself. Granite, breccia, unknown rocks, all may have possibilities for beautiful or unusual surfaces when polished. For example, I have a much admired cabochon of a speckled green stone prised from the surface of a country lane, also some bright red flints and two split-open concretions conveniently brought to the surface in a cemetery. Wherever he may be, the roving eye of the keen lapidary is almost certain to see something of interest. Whether it is something which it is worth while spending time on is another matter, but it will almost certainly find its way to the heap of material which is going to be cut and polished 'one day'.

About two hundred years ago when he and Dr Johnson visited Talisker on the Isle of Skye, Boswell wrote, 'On the shore are many stones full of crystallizations in their hearts'. Perhaps there are some there still.

13 CONFUSION AND DECEPTION

The names given to minerals and gems are often a source of confusion for the man in the street and this is due partly to accident and partly to deliberate intention to deceive. Terms like German Silver or Champagne Cider are deliberately misleading as there is no silver in the first and no champagne in the second. The lapidary may be offered German or Swiss lapis, an inferior stone dyed blue, which someone is trying to pass off as genuine lapis lazuli. This too is a deliberate attempt to deceive the buyer.

Confusion, on the other hand, may occur unwillingly when two different names are used for the same substance, one by mineralogists and another by traders. A typical case is that of aluminium oxide which in its natural state may be called corundum by mineralogists but if it is coloured by trace elements it acquires considerable value and is sold as sapphire or ruby according to the colour.

Confusion can arise when one word is used to denote two quite different things, the word 'carat' being a good example. Precious stones are sold by the carat, which is now universally agreed to be one fifth of a gram. However the word carat, sometimes spelt 'karat', is also used to express the standard of purity of gold. Fine or pure gold is rated as 24 carat gold but as this quality is too soft for many purposes the gold is usually alloyed by mixing it with other metals and the carat number indicates the proportion of gold in the mixture. Eighteen carat gold means 18 parts out of 24 (i.e. $\frac{3}{4}$) are pure gold, and nine carat means that considerably less than half the total is gold—and one wonders why it is still called gold. A mixture of 15 parts polyester and 9 parts cotton certainly could not be sold as nine carat cotton!

To take another example, the word onyx is widely used for two quite different minerals. True onyx is a type of agate with pronounced black and white bands very suitable for cameo carving and it is very hard. In passing one may note that some onyx really is agate but it has been dyed to enhance the contrast; agate can be dyed all sorts of colours. The label 'Genuine onyx' or 'Mexican onyx' can often be seen on ashtrays, book ends etc which are made from a soft variety of banded calcite, and this is not confusion but misrepresentation.

The terms 'rock crystal' or 'crystal' are another puzzle for honest folk who naively assume that things are made from what is on the label. Rock crystal should only be applied to transparent, ice-clear quartz and the museums of

Fig. 86 Fine glass and genuine
rock crystal

the world can show magnificent vases and bowls carved from it with
incredible skill. The Venetians who were, and are, great craftsmen in glass
began to call their clearest quality 'cristallo' with the result that 'crystal' is
now widely used. As glass is an amorphous substance without any
crystalline form the intention is obviously to obtain a high price for the
product by suggesting that it is rock crystal when it is not.

Long ago gems were given names largely on account of their colour and
those found in the Bible or in the Classics do not always correspond with
the gems so called today. Until chemical analysis became possible there
was no way of knowing that a given gem could be several different colours
as well as the one for which it was best known.

It is interesting to go through the list of minerals in Mohs' scale and call
them by more familiar names. Talc is familiar in powdered form, but it is
also another name for mica. Gypsum in certain regions takes on a massive
form which is called alabaster. Calcite, a very common mineral which
exists naturally in a great variety of crystal shapes, is the main ingredient of
limestone and marble.

Fluorite, another common mineral, in crystal form can be transparent,
white, yellow, green, blue, violet or brown. When it wears a blue hat they
call it 'Blue John' in Derbyshire. Apatite and orthoclase come next on the
list, but as neither of these minerals seems to be exploited commercially
they do not sail under any other flag.

Quartz, being hard and plentiful, is used for popular priced jewellery and when it is coloured it is given much more exciting names such as amethyst for the purple, citrine for the yellow and the very misleading 'topaz-quartz' for the sherry coloured. Cairngorm is smoky quartz from Scotland and not from Brazil or anywhere else. The position becomes more complicated with the knowledge that quartz can sometimes be induced to change colour by heat treatment or radiation and only an expert can tell if this has been done. To demonstrate this, put a piece of yellow tiger-eye in a cold oven and heat it up gradually, then switch off and leave it in the oven until it has cooled. It will turn red.

The attractive, deep, sherry colour of some smoky quartz is one which has always been associated with topaz, so much so that everybody knows what colour topaz is. What is much less well known is that real topaz is to be had naturally in many other colours as well as clear, transparent crystals. However, citrine or smoky quartz is so often offered for sale as 'topaz' that the buyer of cut stones or rough material should make quite sure that the seller is offering genuine topaz and not a substitute. The hardness of topaz is 8 against 7 for smoky quartz.

Still under the same heading as quartz comes a whole cluster of minerals in the silica group all made of much the same stuff chemically. It is as though an attractive girl were to change her name with every new dress, so Miss Chalcedony in diaphanous apple green becomes 'Miss Chrysoprase', and in deep red 'Miss Carnelian', whereas the green dress with red spots turns her into 'Miss Heliotrope'—all most confusing. Incidentally she is as hard as flint underneath. Chalcedony is a type of quartz consisting of minute crystals tightly packed together and during formation these crystals become stained different colours. This produces a bewildering variety of types each having a different name. Opaque chalcedony stained red, brown, yellow or a mixture of these is called jasper. If distinct bands of colour form in concentric patterns chalcedony becomes agate, but agate is extremely varied in its appearance giving rise to designations such as lace agate, moss agate, fire agate and so on.

The best way to sort out this puzzle is to find a natural history museum where specimens are well presented and labelled. Also helpful are the excellent books with coloured photographs now on the market.

Another harlequin is tourmaline which can be colourless, green, red, black, brown or blue—and to make things harder a single crystal may be pink at one end and green at the other. Special names have been allocated to different shades of tourmaline, such as rubellite for pink, schorl for black, dravite for brown and quite a few more. On the whole the name tourmaline seems to be reserved for the green kind.

Diamond comes last on Mohs' scale because it is the hardest substance known to man. It consists of pure carbon, and so does graphite with a hardness of less than 2. The lady proudly displaying a magnificent diamond ring would not appreciate being told that it was really the same stuff as chimney soot, yet one cannot cease to wonder at the marvels of nature in giving one substance such contrasting physical properties.

This list by no means covers all the terms which confuse the non-specialist but it should suffice to show that it is wise to deal with a reputable firm and to ask questions when in doubt. It is reasonable to suppose that anyone who sells stones for a living knows more about the game than you do, so if the price is obviously too low there is probably something wrong somewhere. It is either not what it pretends to be, or it has faults in it, or else it has been treated artificially to produce a colour change. Always buy the best quality you can afford from a seller you can trust.

14 FACETING BY HAND

Any amateur who wishes to practise the very rewarding art of hand faceting can easily do so without incurring great expense and without having any previous experience in lapidary work. One does not need to be able to make cabochons before taking up faceting, but two lapidary skills will have to be acquired: dopping and flat lapping on glass. Neither of these takes long to learn. A faceter needs to be able to dop a stone in its proper position, but if dopping with conventional wax proves to be too difficult, the job can be done with modern glues as described in the chapter on dopping.

A very simple device for faceting by hand can soon be made from easily procured and inexpensive materials and no special skills such as cutting threads in metal or silver soldering are needed. Those who have these skills will no doubt use them to improve on the methods of construction described here.

Hand faceting is merely flat lapping stones on sheets of glass using a device—the faceting head—to keep the stone exactly at the desired angle. Figure 87 shows a home-made, complete hand faceting unit. The stone is fixed on the end of a dopstick which can be revolved and then locked in place. The dopstick is gripped in a holder, which in turn is attached to a support which can be freely moved around on a horizontal surface. By altering the difference in height between the base on which the support rests and the glass lap, a facet can be cut with great accuracy at any chosen angle. To do this the stone is held between finger and thumb and ground with a circular motion with loose abrasive grits on the glass lap. Separate sheets of glass are used for different grits and for polishing. The difference in height between the base of the faceting head and the lap determines the angle of the facet, and height is varied by using a series of blocks of chipboard and plywood and sheets of cardboard under the lap or the support for the faceting head. The angle is measured by lining up the dopstick against a free-standing, vertical protractor which is placed behind the lap.

It is of vital importance that the two surfaces, the lap and the support, should at all times be absolutely parallel no matter what the difference in height between them may be. Precision in this is obtained by using blocks of chipboard which, being machine made, are of uniform thickness, and in consequence no great skill is needed to make a hand faceting unit. The

Fig. 87 The home made, hand faceting unit

Fig. 88 Five faceted stones produced with a hand faceting unit

Fig. 89 Plate glass lap, cards, plywood and chipboard blocks, and a shelf resting on a baseboard make up essential elements of a hand faceting unit

113

Fig. 90 Temporary facets cut on the pavilion of an oval stone, according to instructions given in a magazine article. The stone is dopped on a big nail

hand unit has been designed so that all instructions given in books or magazine articles can be followed immediately without any modification or conversion. Moreover if a hand faceter later acquires a machine there will be nothing to unlearn. Home made faceting units are not intended to spoil the sale of faceting machines; on the contrary the idea is to encourage large numbers of people to take up a fascinating new hobby and this will no doubt stimulate interest in faceting machines eventually.

How to use a hand unit

First a suitable piece of faceting grade stone is dopped on the end of the dopstick. The piece of stone should be roughly pre-formed to shape on a wheel or flat lap before faceting begins because this will cut down the work to be done on the faceting laps. Choose a dial setting and lock the dopstick in place by tightening up the wing nut. Set the angle required for the facet on the protractor, rest the stone on a lap and then build up the support until the dopstick is perfectly aligned with the parallel lines of the protractor when it is in the same vertical plane. Grip the stone, not the dopstick, between finger and thumb and move it around on the lap which is covered with grit. Different laps are used for different grades of abrasive or for polishing. When a stone is faceted on a machine it is usual for all the facets to be cut before any of them are polished. A singular advantage of using a hand unit is that a facet can be polished at any time without having to wait until all the others are cut.

Faceted stones have a top and a bottom separated by a girdle at the widest part; these are referred to as the crown and the pavilion. The faceting operation is done in two stages, beginning with the crown or the pavilion, as the worker prefers, and the stone has to be reversed when one end is finished. To do this it is often necessary to use a gadget called a transfer block, which can be bought or made.

Making a hand faceting unit
First method

The faceting head is made up of four main parts, the dopstick, or dop, the dop holder, the dial and the support. It can be made in many different ways according to what comes to hand most readily, and two easily made

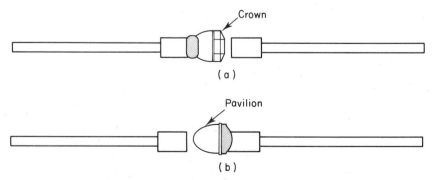

Diag. 22 Reversing the faceted stone by transfer dopping

114

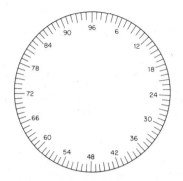

Diag. 23 A 96-division index dial   **Diag. 24** A 64-division index dial

versions are described here. The first one can be made from a pin vice, which can be bought from most good tool shops. The pin vice should be big enough to grip firmly a steel rod 4 mm ($\frac{5}{32}$ in) thick. A threaded bolt or length of threaded rod not less than 4 cm (1$\frac{3}{4}$ in) long, and just thick enough to fit inside the hollow end of the pin vice, is glued in place with epoxy resin. Just under half the length of the bolt should go inside the end of the vice which does not have the gripping part. It must be perfectly aligned, and to do this a length of cotton or thread can be wrapped round the bolt to take up the slack. The head of the bolt is sawn off with a hacksaw when the glue has set. Three ordinary nuts and one wing nut to fit this bolt will be needed as well as a few washers of different sizes.

A dial marked with 96 divisions needs to be fitted on this bolt. Make a drawing or tracing of the ones in diagrams 23, 24 or 42. This dial is protected by a sheet of transparent, rigid plastic cut to the same size. A good size for the dial is a circle with diameter about 7 cm (3 in) if you draw your own. The next thing is to find a strong metal lid which will fit inside the dial without covering the graduations. If the screw-top lid off a glass (jam) jar is too big try one from a small can of paint or baby food. It has to be strong enough not to cave in under pressure and deep enough to accommodate one small nut and washer. Make a hole in the centre, beginning from the inside so that the inevitable burr can be filed away. Instead of metal lids one can use a piece of plywood with a hole in the middle, or even the cover from a bell push.

These different pieces must be threaded on the bolt in the following

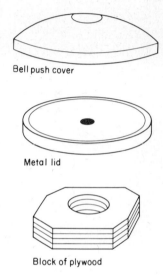

Bell push cover

Metal lid

Block of plywood

Diag. 25 Suitable dial holders

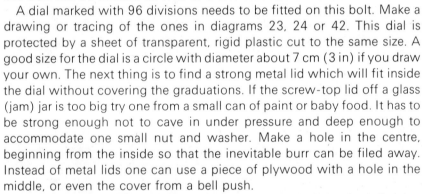

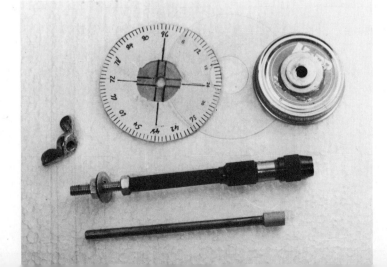

Fig. 91 A pin vice and other pieces used to make a faceting head

115

order: one small nut, one small washer, one big 2 cm (1 in) washer, one metal lid with its top next to the washer, one small washer, one small nut which must be screwed up tight so that the lid cannot move, one disc of transparent plastic, and one paper dial pasted to a sheet of cardboard.

It is of paramount importance for the paper dial to be perfectly centred on the bolt and it is practically impossible to do this by making a suitable hole in the middle of the dial. Start with a piece of stiff card big enough to paste the paper dial on and make a hole in it just big enough for the bolt to pass through. Carefully draw parallel lines on this card at right angles to each other and just touching the bolt (diagram 26). Cut a hole in the centre of the paper dial big enough to push a finger through, and draw two lines at right angles on it from divisions 96 to 48 and from 72 to 24. Put a dab of paste on the back of the dial and centre it so that the diagonals are exactly in the middle of the parallel lines on the card before pasting down the dial all round. This method makes sure that the dial is really centred on the bolt, but if it is not done correctly the faceting will be inaccurate.

Make a hole in the plastic disc about the size of the one in the paper, and then fix it on top of the dial with two or three short strips of cellophane, thread the dial on the bolt and glue the plastic disc to the metal lid. The advantage of doing this is that the cardboard dial can easily be changed for one with 84 divisions or even specially made dials with divisions for cutting gems with 5 or 7 sides instead of the orthodox 8. This is something which is much more difficult to achieve with a machine. When all this has been assembled, the dopholder is complete and ready to be inserted in the support. The bolt goes through a hole in a strip of wood and one more washer and a wing nut are put on and the wing nut tightened up.

Diag. 26 Centring the paper dial round the hole in the card

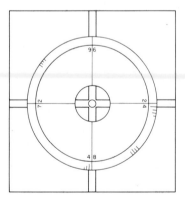

Second method

A different version can be made without using a pin vice, and all that is needed is a length of thin tubing small enough for the steel rod to be a push fit inside it (see figure 92). Brass tubing does very well, but copper bends too easily; you can even use a piece of wood dowelling provided a true hole can be drilled through it. This tube should be about 8 cm (3 in) long and capable of taking a rod not less than 4 mm ($\frac{1}{16}$ in) thick (Meccano axles will do very well) and 12 cm (5 in) long. In the first version the rod is gripped in a pin vice, but in this version it is inserted in the tube until the

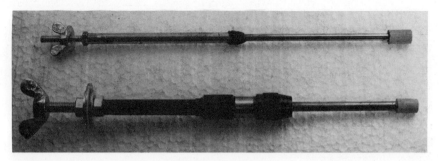

Fig. 92 One version made from a pin vice and another one from a length of brass tube

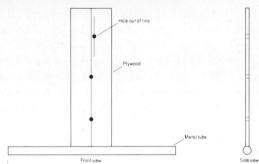

Hole out of line

Plywood

Metal tube

Front view

Side view

Diag. 27 The support for the dop-holder

total length is about 20 cm (8 in) and the two are firmly fixed together by heating up the place where they join and applying a collar of dopwax. This will keep the rod from moving but it can easily be removed by melting the wax when transfer dopping.

Making the support

The support can be made from a strip of multi-ply wood or chipboard thick enough not to bend, about 1 cm ($\frac{3}{8}$ in) and measuring 20 × 6 cm (8 × $2\frac{1}{2}$ in). One end must be quite square because it is to be glued to a length of metal tube 25 cm (10 in) long. The diameter of this tube should be a little bigger than the thickness of the wood so that when the two are glued together the tube will protrude at least on one side. This joint must be done carefully keeping the tube in line with the flat surfaces of the wood. When the glue has set, stand the tube on a flat surface with the wood vertical, then take a set square and draw a thin line up the middle of the wood. Drill three holes on this line in such positions as to allow free rotation of the cardboard dial; in other words the bottom hole will be just over the radius of the dial from the tube and the top hole the same distance from the end of the wood. The measurements will be roughly 4, 10 and 16 cm (1$\frac{5}{8}$, 3$\frac{7}{8}$ and 6$\frac{1}{4}$ in) from the bottom of the wood.

The holes must be big enough for the bolt to go through easily but without excessive play, and they must be drilled straight, perpendicular to the surface. The centre line should pass exactly through the centre of each hole, so if it does not, another line must be drawn through the centre of any hole which happens to be out of line. This is important because this line is the indicator against which the dial is set. When faceting the bolt is put through the bottom hole for angles from 90° to 60°, in the top one for small angles from 0° to 30° and in the middle hole for the rest. Most of the work is done using the middle hole.

Cover the piece of tubing with a piece of thin felt or cloth; flock covered self-adhesive plastic does very well, but make sure that it is of uniform thickness. The purpose of this is to cut down noise and make it easier for the tube to slide over a horizontal surface. When the unit is put to use it will be found that the ends of the tube tend to jump up unless there is sufficient weight, and a weight can be added at the base of the wood where it joins the tube. The size of this weight must be determined by trial and error because too much weight is a nuisance. A piece of lead or stone can be fixed to the wood with adhesive tape, and additional weight added temporarily when cutting a table or star facets because it is when very small angles are being cut that the tube is most likely to jump off the base.

The faceting head is now complete except for the dopsticks, which can be lengths of steel rod. For the pin vice version, lengths of 4 mm ($\frac{1}{8}$ in) rod about 10 cm (4 in) long will be suitable. Whatever is used, the stone when dopped on the end of the dopstick clamped in the middle hole should come not more than 20 cm (8 in) from the tube; this will give ample clearance for moving the stone over the entire lap. If the dop is too long then too many blocks are needed to cut small angles and if it is too short only part of the lap can be used.

The diameter of the end of the dop is the size of the smallest stone which can be faceted, in this case 4 mm ($\frac{1}{8}$ in). However the end of the dopstick can be adapted for larger stones so as to provide a bigger surface for dopping. Find a thin cane of the kind used to support plants but one which has true circular and straight sections. Cut one of these sections into short lengths 1 cm ($\frac{1}{2}$ in) long. If necessary enlarge the hole in the centre so that the steel rod will fit nicely. These short lengths when glued to the end of the rod make excellent dops. They can be made for different pre-forms, a conical depression or a V notch to take pavilions and quite flat for tables. When mounted these pieces of cane can be trued up or reduced in diameter on a grinding wheel. Metal tubing can be used instead of cane but the big advantage of cane is that a stone which has been dopped with alpha glue or epoxy resin can be sawn off the dop with jeweller's saw or a hacksaw when it is held fast in the transfer block. It will not matter if some of the cane is sawn away in the process because a new surface is quickly made with a file or the piece of cane can be replaced.

Baseboard, shelf and blocks

When the faceting head is in use, its base (i.e. the tube) rests on a perfectly flat surface which is either a baseboard or a shelf put on top of it, in which case the shelf must be parallel to it. This base can be a piece of plate glass, or more conveniently a true piece of plastic-coated chipboard thick enough not to warp or bend. A good working size is 35 × 25 cm (14 × 10 in) and 1 cm ($\frac{1}{2}$ in) thick. The shelf can be made from the same material measuring 25 × 16 cm (10 × 6½ in). Also needed are some blocks of uncoated chipboard and plywood, and sheets of cardboard and glass. All these can be rectangles measuring 19 × 16 cm (7½ × 6 in).

To make a shelf take one of these rectangles cut from 2 cm (¾ in) thick, plain chipboard, and also four strips of the same thing 16 cm (6 in) long and 3 cm (1¼ in) wide. The exact width of these strips is not important, nor is great accuracy required in cutting them, the thickness is what matters. Using a very thin film of glue fix these strips to the rectangle, two on each of the short sides; glue the rectangle of coated chipboard centrally on top.

If this is done carefully the shelf unit when completed will be quite parallel to the baseboard when resting on it and the top of the shelf will be about 7 cm (2½ in) above it, depending on the thickness of the chipboards used. Now is the time to measure the height all round to make sure that there is no tilt in any direction, because accurate faceting is impossible if there is any error. The shelf unit will be quite heavy and this is necessary to provide stability when it is propped up on blocks.

In addition to the shelf unit, cut three rectangles from chipboard 2 cm (¾ in) thick, two from chipboard 1 cm (½ in) thick, and two from unwarped plywood about 4 mm ($\frac{3}{16}$ in) thick. Some rectangles of good quality cardboard with a smooth finish are also needed; it is best to buy a sheet of new card for this or to cut up file covers. The thickness of this card should be such that 7 or 8 sheets together are the same thickness as one sheet of plywood. Cut ten rectangles of card. By piling various combinations of wood and card on top of each other it is possible to raise or lower the shelf unit or the glass lap and thereby alter the angle at which the facet is cut. There are enough pieces here to give every angle between 0 and 90 degrees. Obviously there are other ways of achieving the same end but this method has the merit of being simple to make and it works perfectly.

Glass laps are needed for grinding and polishing and time will be saved if a separate one is used for each grade of abrasive. They can be of salvage plate glass or of thick window glass, the important point is that they must all be the same thickness; four will be enough.

Finally some of the same PVC plastic recommended for pebble polishing will also be needed, one rectangle the same size as the glass laps, which incidentally are the same size as the rectangles of wood and card, and another rather larger piece. The smaller piece can be fixed with a dab of glue at each corner to one of the glass laps and this will be used for polishing because most stones can be polished on this type of lap with cerium or tin oxide powder. By fixing the plastic to the glass lap the thickness is increased compared to the other laps, so a spare sheet of PVC must at all times be placed underneath the other laps. This guarantees that the same setting is used when the stone is transferred from a grinding to the polishing lap and it will also help to keep the cards and blocks underneath the laps from being contaminated by loose grit.

Four separate laps take up too much room on any working surface and it is a good idea to fix shelves in a small box and stack up the laps with polish on top and coarse grit at the bottom. Such a box and shelves can be made from cardboard.

Fig. 93 The vertical protractor

Many machine faceters do not use silicon carbide grits but diamond compound. The hand worker will probably already have a stock of grits and it is obviously best for a beginner to start with grit. However, lapping with a hand unit on laps of flat copper and diamond compound is much quicker and cleaner although more expensive. It is something to be kept in mind, and if the hobby is taken up seriously, the switch is easily made. There is so little mess with diamond that one can facet in an ordinary living room without upsetting the mistress of the house.

The vertical protractor

A protractor is needed for measuring the faceting angle; it is not part of the faceting head but stands by itself behind the lap. Find a simple school protractor with easily visible markings and paste it onto a piece of white card. Before doing this it may be necessary to file a small notch in the base of the protractor so that a pin can be put through the card at the exact point which is the centre of the circle from which the protractor is made. Also paste on the card some parallel lines below the base of the protractor (figure 93). These can often be found in writing pads, but they can be drawn with care. With the same centre as the protractor draw a somewhat bigger circle and cut out the card, trimming it close to the edge of the scale. Glue a rectangle of plywood to a base so that it will stand upright, and with great care put a drawing pin through the centre of the card into the plywood. It is important to get this right because the angle will be wrong if the pin is not dead in the centre. Finally turn the disc until the parallel lines are vertical, with the protractor standing on a flat surface; check with a set square and make a small indicator line on the plywood opposite the 0° division. Turn the protractor to 90° and check that the lines are horizontal. In use the protractor is clipped to the plywood with a clothes peg (or clothes pin) once an angle has been selected.

Everything is now ready to facet a simple stone, but usually a transfer block is needed when a stone has to be reversed after cutting one half. Those who are eager to try faceting can cut the first stone selected for an exercise before making a transfer block, or buying one.

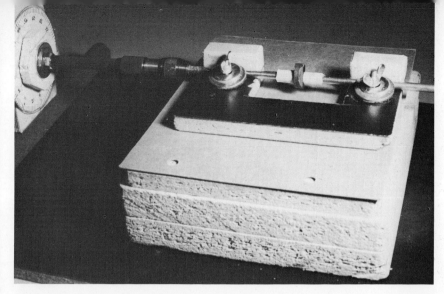

Fig. 94 The transfer block in use

Making a transfer block

For this block two bolts fitted with wing nuts and washers serve to hold two dopsticks firmly in place during the transfer operation. Space is provided for a flame so that dopwax can be used. The dimensions are not critical but the length of the dopstick in use governs the size of the cut-out; the block illustrated is made from a piece of coated chipboard $1 \times 13 \times 8$ cm ($\frac{1}{2} \times 5 \times 3$ in) and the cut-out measures 6×4.5 cm ($2\frac{1}{2} \times 1\frac{3}{4}$ in).

Begin by gluing a strip of wood with a perfectly straight edge along the long side of the base, the straight edge being in the vertical plane facing the base. When the glue has set make the cut-out. This method makes sure of perfect alignment when two dopsticks are put in the block. The hardware consists of two bolts 3 cm ($1\frac{1}{4}$ in) long, each fitted with a wing nut, two small washers, and two big washers 2.5 cm (1 in) across.

Lay the big washers on the base so that they just touch the vertical strip, and drill holes through the base to take the bolts. Countersink the underside of these holes to accommodate the bolt heads, because the base of the block must be quite flat. Fix the bolts in place with a little glue to prevent them from turning. Glue a small washer on top of each big one and a disc of leather underneath; put them over the bolts and add the wing nuts.

In use, both dopsticks are held tight in the angle between the base of the block and the strip of wood by pressure from the big washers when the wing nuts are screwed tight, and they will be in perfect alignment.

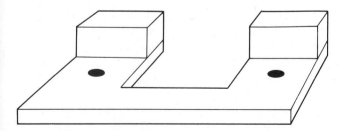

Diag. 28 The transfer block ready for the bolts

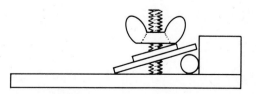

Diag. 29 The end view of the transfer block

Fig. 95 *Left:* The crown of a cut corner square stone

Fig. 96 *Right:* Pavilion of the same stone with eight facets converging to a single point

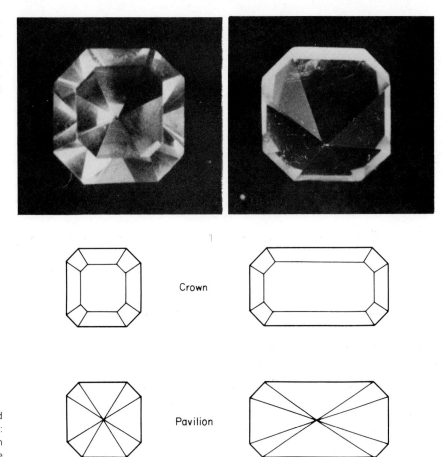

Crown

Pavilion

Diag. 30 Square and rectangular cut corner stones: the table is a little more than half the width of the stone

Faceting a square or rectangular stone with cut corners

A square or a rectangle with cut corners is a good shape to choose for a first attempt at faceting a stone by hand, one advantage being that no transfer block is required. It is foolish to waste good faceting material, so do not grind down a piece of rough to make a square if it will make a bigger rectangular stone. Any member of the quartz family is good for beginners, preferably a coloured one like amethyst or citrine. Examine the stone carefully under a bright light to make sure there are no internal cracks or blemishes; in the case of amethyst look for where the colour is deepest and arrange for this part to be at the bottom of the stone.

Although a hand faceter does not need to be able to make cabochons on a grinding wheel it is an advantage to be able to make pre-forms. This means grinding away excess material with a wheel so that not very much is left to be removed on the faceting lap. The pre-form has to be carefully judged because it is easy to cut away too much and then there is nothing left to facet in some places. If no grinding wheel is available then pre-form by flat lapping on a large sheet of glass with coarse (100) grit, dopping the stone temporarily if it is difficult to hold. For a square stone the piece of rough should be a cube which can be preformed. For this exercise the finished stone can be approximately 12 mm ($\frac{1}{2}$ in) square by 10 mm ($\frac{2}{5}$ in) deep and a table width of 8 mm ($\frac{3}{8}$ in) and an extra wide girdle up to 2 mm ($\frac{1}{16}$ in). These measurements are merely an indication, as the size of the stone will depend on the size of the piece of rough.

Begin by grinding a small flat surface where the table will be and dop the stone on this table temporarily so that it can be pre-formed. After pre-forming, mark out the size of the table with an aluminium pencil. The stone is going to have cut corners so if it is ground as a square now it will be smaller than it need be. With a little ingenuity a bigger stone can be obtained as shown in diagram 31. What is marked out is the overall size of

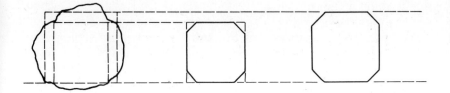

Diag. 31 With a little ingenuity, a bigger stone can be obtained

the finished stone when measured at the girdle. Make a cross with the pencil at the centre of the stone.

The next operation is to put the stone on the faceting dop, but the end of two dops should be trued up first. Put the dop-holder in the top hole of the faceting head and push the dop into it as far as it will go before tightening up. Lay a sheet of abrasive paper on a glass lap on the baseboard, then build up the shelf on blocks and cards until the dopstick is quite perpendicular to the lap, and true the end by rubbing it on the abrasive paper. Do the same for a second dop. Later, when the stone is dopped this is the position for lapping the table.

Remove the lap and put a sheet of plain paper on the baseboard with two lines intersecting at right angles drawn on it. Put the stone, flat side down

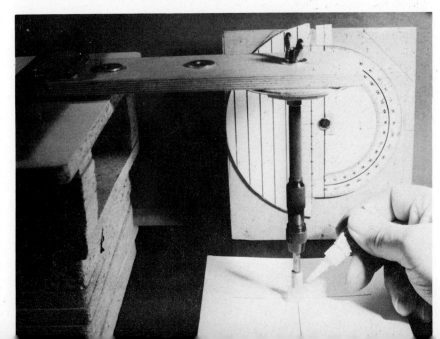

Fig. 97 Fixing a pre-formed stone to the dop with alpha glue

123

on the paper with the centre at the intersection of the lines and then position the dopstick exactly over the centre. The shelf will need to be raised by the same amount as the thickness of the stone to bring the dopstick perpendicular once more. It is not at all easy to dop the stone so that it is centred on the dop and if dop wax is used one cannot see clearly. A simple solution to the problem is to secure the stone with one or two drops of alpha glue and wait for it to set.

Remove the sheet of paper and replace it by a sheet of PVC plastic on top of which is a glass lap with 300 grit; adjust the shelf so that the dopstick is once again perpendicular to the lap. It must be kept in mind at all stages of lapping and polishing that as the surface of a facet is worn down the angle of the dopstick will alter slightly. This applies to all angles, even 90°, so keep an eye on the protractor and add a card underneath the lap to make sure that the angle is correct if there has been any significant deviation.

When the table is judged to be wide enough—at this stage it should be about two thirds the width of the stone—finish it on fine grit and aluminium oxide and it is ready for polishing. One way is to take the dop out of the pin vice and polish the table on a felt pad on the grinding wheel; this will produce rounded edges, but they will disappear later on when the crown main facets cut into the table. The alternative is to change the lap for a polishing lap, not forgetting to remove the extra sheet of PVC, and polish on the lap. Before doing this chamfer the edges of the stone slightly with a piece of abrasive paper to prevent tiny particles from breaking away from the edge and scratching the stone.

When the table has been polished to satisfaction without any hairline scratches the stone can be 'squared'. This term is used even though the

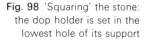

Fig. 98 'Squaring' the stone: the dop holder is set in the lowest hole of its support

stone may be a round one and it means forming a girdle at 90° to the table. Return the dopstick to the pin vice, but in the fully extended position this time, and set the protractor at 90°. The dopstick is best put in the bottom hole for this operation and the dial set at 96 and screwed up tight. Rotate the stone until the part which is to form one side is in contact with a grinding lap which has been built up so that the dopstick is exactly horizontal when the stone rests on it. Tighten the pin vice well because the stone will remain like this in relation to the dopstick and dial until the crown is finished. Proceed to grind one side at the 96 setting, adding a card or cards as necessary to keep the dopstick horizontal; do this with 300 grit.

When the side is judged to be long enough, change the dial setting to 48 and cut the opposite side parallel to the first one, always making the necessary adjustments by adding or taking away a card or two. Cut the two remaining sides at settings 72 and 24, whether the stone is to be a square or a rectangle. In the case of a rectangle begin with the long sides first. It is most unlikely that the stone will have been dopped so that the centre now corresponds with the centre of the dop, but this does not matter. All that happens is that the sides will not be equidistant from the centre and that no height setting can be taken for granted. The angle must be checked each time and the only thing that does matter is to make sure that opposite sides are parallel to each other.

This is the moment to check that the apparatus has been made and assembled correctly. If two sides are not quite parallel to each other, or if adjacent sides are not at right angles, the trouble can be caused by one of four things. The shelf may be lower at one end than the other, the dial may not be centred on the bolt, the indicator line for dial settings may not be

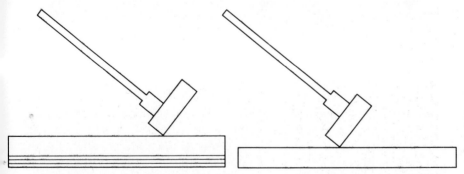

Diag. 32 The stone is not centred on the dop so for a constant angle the height setting must be checked each time

above the centre of the hole where the bolt goes, and lastly the hole may be out of true. It is assumed that the dial settings have been made with care, because this is the obvious source of error due to careless working rather than faulty apparatus. The reason for choosing a square stone for the first attempt is that it is the best shape for checking the gear. It would be much more difficult to spot any fault if the first cut were to be a standard brilliant.

Assuming that all is well or that any necessary adjustments have been made, the next step is to cut the corners, with the dopstick always horizontal, at settings 60, 12, 84 and 36, making sure that they are all the same length so that the final shape is symmetrical. Do this with 300 grit as

125

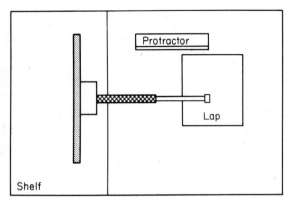

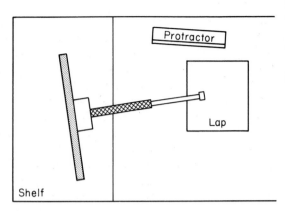

Diag. 33 Sighting the angle: correct position   **Diag. 34** Sighting the angle: wrong position

there is no point in using a finer one at this stage. The stone has now been 'squared', and although part of the eight surfaces which have been ground will be cut away in subsequent faceting, a narrow band will remain as the girdle of the finished stone.

The next operation is to cut the crown main facets, which in this instance are the only crown facets, and for this the dopstick is removed to the middle hole in the support, which should be raised up on the shelf. Set the dial to 96 and the angle to 45°, use cards and blocks to adjust the relative height between shelf and lap and with the stone resting on the lap sight the dopstick against the protractor to make sure it is at the proper angle. When doing this the angle will not be true unless the tube of the faceting head is at right angles to the face of the protractor, which in turn should be positioned squarely behind the lap (diagram 33).

Make allowance for a change in the angle as the stone is ground away by starting at a slightly higher angle than the final 45°. This is something which becomes easier as one gains experience. It is all too easy for a faceter to make mistakes in settings, and a golden rule is to grind very little before looking at the stone to see that all is well. If a mistake has been made it can often be retrieved if cutting has not gone very far; otherwise all the work may have to be done again. Another practice which can be strongly recommended is to keep a log of every stone cut and note down each stage so that if work is interrupted it can be taken up again without difficulty. It is impossible to remember dial and angle settings. An example of a log entry might read like this

Crown mains	45	96	48	72	24	60	12	82	36
Cut			✓	✓	✓	✓	✓	✓	✓ ✓
Polished		✓	✓	✓					

with a tick put against each setting as the facet is cut or polished.

Start grinding the first crown facet on 300 grit with frequent checks to see how it is going, because this is the point where a final check on the accuracy of the apparatus can most easily be made. If the two sides of this crown facet are not parallel when the dial setting is correctly made one must re-check the gear. Once satisfied that everything is in order, there is no need to be concerned any more with this problem, and complicated cuts of all kinds may be attempted with confidence.

Cleanliness is important because loose grit or any other foreign body between the blocks and cards will throw the facets out of true. Lapping with 300 grit leaves a ragged edge to the facet so cutting should be stopped short of the final position and the facet finished on 400 grit and aluminium oxide, cleaning the stone between each transfer to another lap. Remember that even polishing has an abrasive action which very slightly increases the size of a facet. The width of the crown facets is a matter of personal choice; the wider they become the smaller will be the table of the finished stone. For a square stone the table can be a little more than half the total width, and similarly for a rectangular one.

After having begun the first facet at 96, turn the dial to 48 and cut a similar one opposite before returning once more to 96. Continue cutting first one side and then the other until satisfied with the proportions obtained. Of course these two facets must be exactly the same width. With an aluminium pencil mark a line at the bottom edge of these two facets and continue this line right round the stone. This line constitutes the top edge of the girdle and the remaining six crown facets, all cut at 45°, must just reach the girdle line.

The dial settings for these crown facets are the same ones used for squaring the stone, namely 96, 48, 72, 24, 60, 12, 84, 36. Before the facets reach the line the laps are changed to finer grits, but very little rubbing on 400 grit and aluminium oxide need be done because these last two are a preparation for polishing rather than a means of removing material. Ideally all eight facets should be exactly the same width and have parallel sides; where two facets meet the girdle all four surfaces should meet in one point

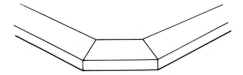

Diag. 35 Four facets meeting in a point

(diagram 35). This is the test of a good faceter and the beginner will not have perfect meets if the work is carelessly done. A good magnifying glass or a jeweller's loupe is needed for examining progress in detail and for spotting scratches when polishing.

Before the corner facets are completed it may be necessary to alter the dial setting fractionally to make sure of a good meet. Work slowly and carefully to avoid mistakes, for the fact that one is using home-made equipment is no excuse for shoddy work; the target must always be perfection.

With practice it is possible to achieve perfection but it will not come right away, the dial setting may have been slightly to one side of the indicator, or

Fig. 99 'Cheating' with a card
slipped between one side of
the shelf and the baseboard

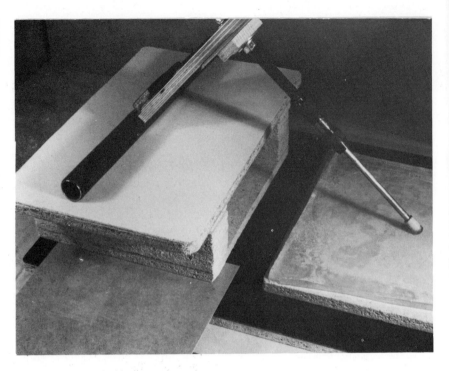

perhaps too much pressure was applied to one side of the stone when lapping. Fortunately there is a way of correcting slight errors by a form of cheating. If two sides of a facet are very nearly parallel but not quite, a minute adjustment in the dial setting can be made, but it is much easier to cheat by slipping the edge of a sheet of card under one end of the shelf (diagram 36). This is a bad habit which should be avoided as much as possible, but it is extremely useful for very small corrections, especially when cutting a standard brilliant or the narrow facets of a step cut stone. Very often a facet when polished may have a dull spot at one extreme which can be polished by cheating.

When the crown facets are ready to be polished, remove the sheet of PVC which has been put under the cutting laps, and put the polishing lap in place. As this lap has a sheet of the same PVC on top the height setting will remain the same. Put a very weak mixture of cerium oxide and pure water on the lap and test with the ball of a finger to make sure there are no hard particles or dry patches present. This has to be done regularly because a thin film of water soon evaporates and leaves dry powder round the

Diag. 36 'Cheating' with a card

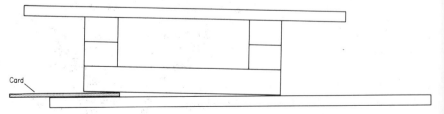

Card

edges. A stone rubbed on dry polishing powder will be scratched immediately.

Faceting books usually recommend a light touch for polishing, but when polishing by hand on PVC sheet it will be found that considerable pressure and a few rapid movements over a small area will quickly polish a small facet. The worker has to experiment with different pressures and movements to find what brings the best results. The water must be free from foreign matter and experiments with different detergents or softeners in minute quantity may well improve performance.

The crown of the stone is finished when the table and main facets have been polished and a transfer operation has to be carried out before cutting the pavilion. In this particular case there is no need for a transfer block, indeed if the stone is not centred on the dopstick the error will only be repeated if a transfer block is used. Cut the stone off the dop with a small saw and clean it in acetone to remove any remaining glue. Once again put the sheet of paper with intersecting lines on it on the baseboard and centre the stone table upwards, supporting it with wax or plasticine. Fix it to the second dopstick in exactly the same way as before with a drop or two of alpha glue, and wait patiently until it has set hard enough for work to begin again.

With the dopstick in the lowest hole of the support and in a horizontal position, lay one edge of the stone firmly against a lap at the correct height and tighten up the pin vice. If the dial is set firmly at 96 when doing this the pavilion facets are bound to come opposite the crown facets. This procedure is valid for fair sized square or rectangular stones, but other types will need to be reversed in a transfer block. When a transfer block is used, the stone must not be cut away from the first dop before it is firmly secured to the second one.

The pavilion of this stone is going to be a pyramid with eight sides each of which corresponds to a crown facet and all meeting in a central point. For a first attempt allow for an extra wide girdle of 1.5 mm or more as this gives more scope for correcting any unfortunate mistakes. There are rigid optical laws governing the facet angles which produce maximum brilliance for any given mineral. These angles can be found in faceting manuals and in the case of various forms of quartz the angles recommended are from 41° to 43° for pavilion main facets, depending on whether the quartz is clear or coloured. If amethyst is used the facets can be cut at 43°.

Fix the dop-holder in the middle hole with the dial setting 96 and the protractor set at 43°, build up the lap, not forgetting to put the loose sheet of PVC underneath, and grind a facet on 300 grit until it leaves a girdle of the desired width. Change the setting to 48 and cut the opposite side. These two facets, if correctly cut, should meet in a knife edge exactly below the centre of the stone and the girdle width at the base of each facet should be the same.

Proceed to cut the next two facets at settings 72 and 24 so that all four meet in a central point and then finish these four facets on 400 grit. Return to 300 grit and cut the four remaining facets at 84, 36, 60, 12 settings and finish them on fine grit. Polish all these eight facets and then the girdle. The stone is finished, so cut it off the dop and clean it up.

Great joy and satisfaction can be had from exhibiting the first faceted gem you have ever made with your own hands, and it is something well within the reach of far more people than is generally realised.

The emerald or step cut

This cut, very popular for jewellery, is usually considered to be too difficult for beginners because a rotating lap cuts faster on the outside than it does in the middle, which does not help one to cut parallel edges. This problem does not arise when lapping by hand, nevertheless a step cut is a tough test of skill. Choose a fairly dark coloured stone such as smoky quartz and grind it to a pre-form. In this exercise make a rectangular stone about twice as long as it is wide with a crown similar to the previous stone. The more ambitious can cut an extra set of facets on the crown between the main facets and the table. If the mains are cut at an angle of 45° the extra ones can be cut at 30°. They are cut at the same settings as the mains but should be much narrower, not more than half the width of the mains when the stone is finished. There will be a series of facets cut in three steps on the pavilion and it is important to make sure that there is enough material to make these steps. The pre-form when seen from the end should have a bulge at the girdle and the sides must not be too straight (diagram 37).

For step cut stones the main pavilion facets, that is to say, the ones cut at the correct angle for maximum brilliance, are the ones at the very bottom, and in the case of smoky quartz they will be at 43°. However pavilion facets have to be cut beginning at the girdle, so angles have to be determined for the two sets of facets which will be cut before the mains. The number of steps which can be cut in a stone is governed by the amount of material available below the girdle and the angle between the steps. All these things are explained in faceting manuals, but in this case let the depth of the pavilion when measured from the girdle be twice the depth of the crown, and there will be room to cut three steps at angles 55°, 49° and 43°, beginning with the one next to the girdle. When the crown has been cut and the stone transferred to another dop, set the dial at 96 and cut a facet in line with its corresponding crown facet at 55° on 300 grit so that its edges

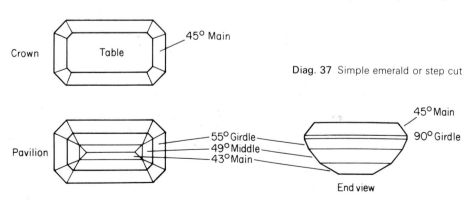

Crown   Table   45° Main

Diag. 37 Simple emerald or step cut

Pavilion   55° Girdle   49° Middle   43° Main   45° Main   90° Girdle

End view

are parallel and also parallel to the girdle line of the crown.

Continue cutting this facet until it is about half the total depth of the pavilion, then with the same setting 96, change the angle to 49°, and cut another facet next to it, and after that a third facet at 43°. Do not finish any of these facets yet. For a neat stone they should all appear to be the same width when viewed from above, but because of foreshortening they will not be of equal width and so they have to be cut a little at a time until a satisfactory balance is obtained.

Change the dial setting to 48 and repeat the process on the opposite side of the stone, making sure that the main facets at the bottom meet in a knife edge down the centre. Cut similar facets at the two ends of the stone with settings 72 and 24, taking care to make them the same width as the others. Go over all these facets on the 400 grit lap until they come out right and then polish them. This leaves the corner facets uncompleted, and they have to be cut and polished at settings 84, 60, 36, 12, but there will only be two steps at 55° and 49° by which time they run to a point, or nearly so, and there is nothing left to cut main facets at the corners.

This produces a very elementary step cut stone, and a second attempt should be made to cut one with four steps. In the first case the three steps were cut at angles which differed by 6°, and if four steps are made this can be increased to 7°, which gives angles of 64, 57, 50, and 43 degrees for smoky quartz, the 64° coming next to the girdle. The pavilion can be not quite so deep in proportion to the crown as it was for a three-step stone.

The standard brilliant cut

For this exercise a piece of clear quartz is needed, large enough to make a stone some 8 or 10 mm ($\frac{3}{8}$ in) across. Begin by pre-forming the rough, which can be done on a hand wheel using the jig described in chapter 11. For a brilliant cut stone the pre-form is circular in cross section at all points, and it should be rather like a radish with sides that bulge and not like a carrot (diagram 39). The pre-form can be put on a faceting dop which has been recessed as this will give more security than one with a flat end.

Diag. 39 Side view of standard brilliant cut

Diag. 38 Standard brilliant cut

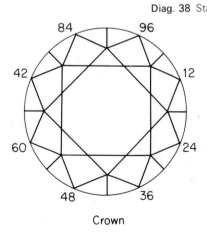

Crown

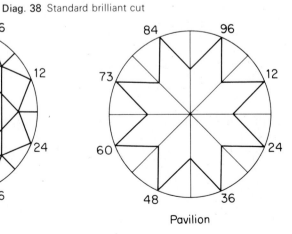

Pavilion

Use the technique already described to cut and polish a table which at this stage should be at least two thirds the width of the stone because it will decrease in size when facets are cut into it. Cut eight main crown facets of equal width at settings 96, 48, 24, 72, 12, 36, 60, 84, and angle 42°, in that order, the first pairs being cut alternately a little at a time until the width of the table can be ascertained.

When the first four facets are deep enough and all the same size, cut the remaining four, and finish them on the finer grits so that they form an even girdle line. It is much easier to polish them all now than to return later and have to find the setting again.

The star or table facets are the next ones to cut and as they are small this should be done with 400 grit and with great caution. There are eight of these facets, triangular in shape with the points downwards, and they are cut at settings 6, 18, 30, 42, 54, 60, 78, 90, so that when completed the base of each triangle just touches its neighbours on either side and the point reaches down one third of the length of the line where two main facets come together.

It is usual to cut star facets at an angle of 15° smaller than the angle of the main facets, but this is only a figure for guidance and the exact angle has to be found by trial and error since it varies with the size of the stone. If the mains were cut at 45° the protractor must be set at 30° to start with and the lap should have one thin piece of plywood and four or five cards beneath it when the dopstick is lined up properly. The reason for this is that the angle is going to be progressively reduced until the right one is found, and it is much easier to remove cards from under the lap than to add them below the shelf. Angles are reduced by increasing the difference in height between shelf and lap.

To cut the star facets, put the dop-holder in the top hole of the faceting head. Begin with the dial at 6 and cut a very small facet on 400 grit. Move the dial to 18 and cut another one, then go back to 6 and cut a little more and so on. By doing this it is possible to estimate whether the point of the triangle is going to reach down to about one third of the depth of the main facets by the time its base spreads far enough to touch its neighbour. At an angle of 30 the point will probably not go down far enough, so the angle has to be reduced. Take away a card from under the lap and try again but if the facets are growing too big stop cutting them and move to another pair at settings 30 and 42, leaving the first two to be completed later on.

Continue this process, taking away cards and if necessary moving on to the next pair of settings 54 and 66 until the right angle has been found, and set the protractor at this angle which may be 28° or 27° or even less. As soon as a pair of facets come out right they can be polished, and without any further adjustments all the other star facets can be finished and polished, including those which have been partly cut when establishing the proper setting. If one persists in trying to find the necessary angle with the first pair of facets they will inevitably be overcut, and this means that all the main facets will have to be re-cut.

Whenever a setting needs to be recorded for reference it is a good plan to put down not only the angle but also what blocks and cards were used.

This can be done in a kind of shorthand where 96, 43—S, 0, 0, 1, 3/L, 2, 1, 0, 0 stands for a dial setting and angle with the shelf supported by one sheet of thin ply and three cards and the lap supported by two blocks of 2 cm ($\frac{3}{4}$ in) and one block of 1 cm ($\frac{1}{2}$ in) blockboard, no ply and no cards. It is much easier to go back to a setting recorded like this than to find an angle exactly.

Sixteen crown girdle facets have to be cut next at settings 3, 9, 15, 21, 27, 33, 39, 45, 51, 63, 69, 75, 81, 87, 93. Their position is at the base of the main facets, and their bases form a line at the upper edge of the girdle, whilst their points reach up two thirds of the length of the main facets until they meet the points of the star facets. In principle these facets are cut at an angle 5° bigger than that used for the mains, but in fact the same process has to be used as for cutting the star facets. Set the protractor to 47° and start cutting facets at settings 3 and 9. If the point of the facets seems to be running up too fast compared with the spread of the base, then the angle needs to be increased by adding cards under the lap. On the other hand if the point is going to be too short when the bases meet, take away cards to reduce the angle. Most probably the angle will need to be increased. Keep moving on to new pairs of facets until the right angle has been found and then finish all sixteen, polishing as you go. This completes the crown.

Transfer dopping

Transfer dopping is needed to make a standard brilliant. When the crown is complete put the dop-holder in the bottom hole of the support with the dial set at 96, and clamp the dopstick in one side of the transfer block, which needs to be supported on blocks so that the dopstick is quite horizontal. Clamp a new dop in the other side of the block and glue the stone to it before cutting the first dop free. Unscrew the pin vice, take the dop-holder round to the new dop and fix it firmly in place; this is the reason for having a transfer block with a flat base raised to the necessary height for the changeover. If the operation is carried out carefully the pavilion facets are bound to coincide with the crown facets and there will be no need for any adjustment to be made, but it is prudent to check as soon as one starts cutting the first pavilion facet.

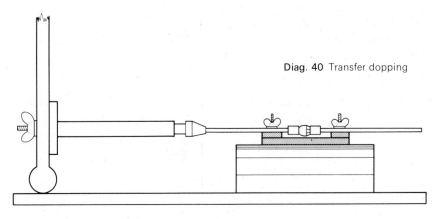

Diag. 40 Transfer dopping

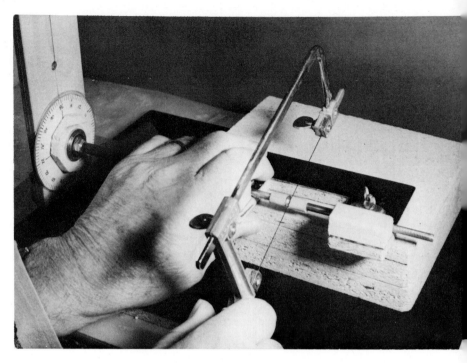

Cut a little of the first pavilion facet with the dial set at 96 and examine the stone carefully to make sure that it really does coincide with the crown facet above it. If there is any deviation the dop can be loosened in the pin vice and a small rotation made to bring the facets into line. There is an alternative method which is easier to do and it consists in making a temporary index for the dial setting. Turn the dial either to the right or the left of the normal index mark until the pavilion facet is lined up with the corresponding crown facet. The 96 mark on the dial will no longer be

Diag. 41 Using a temporary index mark for a small correction to the dial setting

Diag. 42 (Far right) Actual size conversion table for faceting dials with 96 or 64 divisions

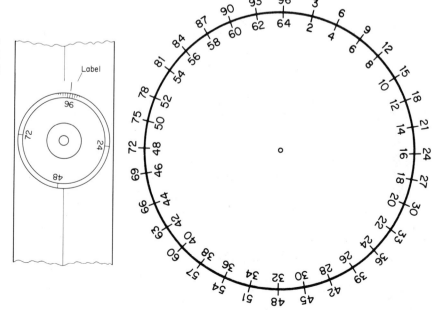

opposite the index mark. Stick a small self-adhesive label over the index mark and draw a new mark on the label opposite the 96 division on the dial. Use this temporary index mark for all the remaining facets and they will come out correctly. Remove the label when the stone is finished.

With the dop-holder in the middle hole, cut eight pavilion main facets at 41°, using the same index settings as for the crown main facets. These facets are taken down to the girdle, but do not make the girdle too thin because it will tend to chip when the stone is mounted. Cut and polish all eight pavilion mains and then start on the pavilion girdle facets. These are the last ones and they are cut in exactly the same way as the crown girdle facets and at the same settings, but in this case the points should be made to reach half way down the main pavilion facets, rather more than less. Once again the correct angle needs to be found by trial and error starting with an angle only 2 degrees more than the 41° used for the pavilion mains and increasing it gradually by adding cards underneath the lap. When these facets are cut and polished the stone is complete except for polishing the girdle.

Remove the dopstick from the faceting head, and polish the girdle by holding it in the hand and rotating the stone on a polishing lap with the dop held horizontally. Cut the stone off the dop and clean it in acetone before deciding how you can do better next time.

Modified standard brilliant

The hand faceter who does not have a grinding wheel cannot easily make the circular pre-form for a standard brilliant cut, but a modified shape with sixteen facets round the girdle can be made entirely by flat lapping. Begin as before with a flat surface for the table and the stone dopped on it as centrally as can be managed. With the dop-holder in the bottom hole, and an angle of 90°, lap four flat surfaces at 96, 48, 72, 24 so that they are all equidistant from the centre, but do not complete the square which is being formed because this will waste material. Lap four more flat surfaces at 12, 60, 84, 36 to make a regular octagon.

When satisfied that all these surfaces are the same width, cut smaller surfaces also of equal width using settings 3, 9, 15, 21, 27, 33, 39, 45, 51, 63, 69, 75, 81, 87, 93 to produce a regular prism with sixteen sides. Cut a standard brilliant from this prism as before; the only difference will be a girdle with sixteen facets instead of a circular one.

The instructions given here will enable the hand faceter to make a start, but for more advanced work and for different minerals it is essential to have more information. Quartz only has been suggested so far because it has the merit of being attractive, easily obtained, inexpensive, not too hard and it has no cleavage. However there is no reason why a beginner should not try a piece of almandine garnet or aquamarine. This type of garnet is usually deep red in colour, the same hardness as quartz, with a refractive index somewhat higher. This means that the angles will differ, so the crown mains must be cut at 37° and the pavilion mains at 42° with corresponding alterations for the star and girdle facets.

Garnet has superior dispersion to quartz, which gives a brighter finished stone, and more sparkle than quartz. Aquamarine is a very pretty mineral and faceting grade of good colour is expensive, but sometimes one can find small pieces free from flaws which have been tumbled and small brilliants can be made from them. It is slightly harder than quartz, but the refractive index is so close that the same angles can be used as for quartz.

Conclusion

This book will have achieved its objective if the joy and satisfaction of creative lapidary work can be introduced to many more people than those who enjoy it today. By making a modest start with simple apparatus, working only by hand, it is possible to accomplish much more than one imagines. In the case of young people, new and fascinating horizons in related fields can be opened up by an initial interest in working simple stones.

GLOSSARY

Adularescence A milky or bluish sheen in gemstones, particularly feldspars.

Amber A fossil resin, found on the shores of the Baltic Sea.

Asterism An effect of light, displaying rayed star formations, due to the presence of minute inclusions arranged in a regular series in some varieties of ruby, sapphire, phlogopite mica etc.

Boulder clay Deposit of clay from the Ice Age containing boulders and pebbles.

Brilliant A type of cut originally designed for diamonds. It has 57 facets, or 58 if the point is flattened to a culet.

Cabochon A stone which is cut 'en cabochon' is domed like the top of a human head. It has no facets, and its outline may be circular, oval or elliptical.

Cameo A stone or shell in two or more layers of different shades on which figures are carved in relief.

Carat The weight of a precious stone: one carat equals a fifth of a gram. For metals, a carat (or karat) is one 24th part of the whole (e.g. 18 carat gold denotes that 18/24ths of the alloy are pure gold).

Carnelian A translucent, red-coloured type of chalcedony.

Chalcedony A crypto-crystalline form of quartz.

Chatoyancy Optical effect shown by cat's-eye and other stones due to the reflection of light from minute aligned tubular fibres. When cut 'en cabochon' such stones exhibit a narrow band of light which changes its position as the stone is turned.

Conchoidal Showing shell-like surfaces after fracture.

Concretion A mass of solid particles formed round a nucleus.

Crown The top half of a faceted stone.

Culet The facet at the back point of the stone.

Dichroic Showing two different colours.

Dopping When a stone is dopped, it is fixed with wax or other adhesives to a short stick for easier manipulation.

Faceting Cutting flat faces on a stone.

Flat lapping Grinding or polishing a stone on a flat, horizontal plate.

Flint A very hard stone made of silica.

Geode A nodule of stone, hollow in the middle and usually containing crystals.

Hardness Resistance to scratching.

Igneous Rocks of volcanic origin.

Inclusions Small bodies encased in larger masses of mineral.

Intaglio A carving incised or engraved in stone.

Iridescence The production of fine (rainbow) colours on a surface due to the interference of light reflected from the front and back of a very thin film.

Lap The flat plate on which a stone is ground or polished.

Lapidary (Noun) Person who cuts, polishes or engraves precious stones.
   (Adjective) Concerned with precious stones.

Linde 'A' Trade name for an extremely fine grade of aluminium oxide.

Loupe High-powered magnifying glass which fits in the eye socket.

Lustre The light reflected from the surface of a mineral. The highest degree of lustre in opaque minerals is 'splendent', and in transparent minerals is 'adamantine' (i.e. the lustre of a diamond); 'metallic' and 'vitreous' are less brilliant, while 'pearly', 'resinous' and 'dull' have a low degree of lustre.

Metamorphic Rock which has changed its nature on account of great heat or pressure or both.

Mica A silicate which forms in glittering scales or crystals.

Mohs' scale Internationally accepted scale of measuring hardness of stones, drawn up by Friedrich Mohs in 1822.

Netsuke Small, carved, decorative ornament worn by Japanese.

Obsidian Type of volcanic glass.

Opalescence Milky effect due to scattering of light from small particles (as in the opal).

Orienting Positioning a stone in a definite plane.

Orthoclase-feldspar A silicate of aluminium and potassium.

Pavilion The bottom part of a faceted stone which lies below the girdle.

Pleochroic Showing different colours when viewed from different sides.

Pre-form Material roughly ground to shape ready for faceting.

Refraction A change in the direction of propagation of a wavefront when a wave (of light, for example) crosses a boundary between two media in which its phase velocity differs (e.g. when a stick half submerged in water appears to be bent).

Rock crystal Colourless quartz.

Sanding Smoothing the surface of a stone with abrasive paper or cloth.

Schiller Planes of reflected light from cleavage layers.

Sedimentary Rocks formed by the deposition of sediment.

Stromatolite In layers like bedclothes.

Table The large facet on the top of a stone.

Vitreous Like glass in hardness, brittleness, transparency or structure.

BIBLIOGRAPHY

Allen, J, *Guide to Craft Suppliers*, Studio Vista, 1974

Edwards, R, *The Technique of Jewellery*, Batsford, London, 1977

Hoffman, D L, *Comprehensive Faceting Instructions*, Aurora Lapidary Books, USA 1968

Kirkaldy, J F, *Minerals and Rocks in Colour*, Blandford Press, London 1963

Quick, L, and Leiper, H., *Gemcraft*, Pitman, London, and Chilton, Philadelphia, 1960

Rodgers, P, *Agate Collecting in Britain*, Batsford 1975

Scarfe, H, *Collecting and Polishing Stones*, Batsford, London, 1973

Scarfe, H, *Cutting and Setting Stones*, Batsford, London, 1972

Scarfe, H, *The Lapidary Manual*, Batsford, London, 1975

Scarfe, H, *Advanced Lapidary Techniques*, Batsford, 1979

Sinkankas, J, *Gemstones of North America*, Van Nostrand Co, New York, 1972

Sinkankas, J, *Standard Catalogue of Gems*, Van Nostrand Co, New York, 1968

Smith, H G F, *Gemstones*, Chapman & Hall, London, 1973

Webster, R, *Gems, Their Sources, Descriptions and Identification*, Butterworth, London, and Shoe String, Connecticut, 1962

Magazines

Gems, (bi-monthly) Lapidary Publications, 7 Hillingdon Avenue, Sevenoaks, Kent

Gem Craft, (monthly) Model and Allied Publications Ltd, P. O. Box 35, Bridge Street, Hemel Hempstead, Herts., England

Gems and Minerals, (monthly) Gemac Corporation, P.O. Box 687, Mentone, California, USA

Lapidary Journal, (monthly) P.O. Box 80937, San Diego, California, USA

Rock and Gem, (bi-monthly) Behn-Miller Publishers Inc., 16250 Ventura Blvd., Encino, California, USA

The Canadian Rockhound, (bi-monthly) 941 Wavertree Road, North Vancouver, British Columbia, Canada

Australian Lapidary Magazine, (bi-monthly) Jay Kay Publications, 11 Robinson Street, Sydney, N.S.W., Australia

LIST OF SUPPLIERS

UK

Ammonite Ltd, Llandow, Cowbridge, Glamorgan, Wales
M. L. Beach (Products) Ltd, 41 Church Street, Twickenham, Middlesex
Caverswall Minerals, The Dams, Caverswall, Stoke-on-Trent, Staffs.
Craftorama, 14 Endell Street, London WC2
Gemrocks Ltd., 7 Brunswick Shopping Centre, London WC1
Derwent Crafts, 50 Stonegate, York
Gemset of Broadstairs Ltd, 31 Albion Street, Broadstairs, Kent
Gemstones Limited, 44 Walmsley Street, Hull, North Humberside
Glenjoy Lapidary Supplies, 19/21 Sun Lane, Wakefield, Yorkshire
Hirsh Jacobson Merchandising Co. Ltd, 91 Marylebone High Street,
    London W1
Kernowcraft Rocks & Gems Ltd, 44 Lemon Street, Truro, Cornwall
Manchester Minerals, 33 School Lane, Heaton Chapel, Stockport, Cheshire
A. Massie & Son, 158 Burgoyne Road, Sheffield 6, Yorkshire
PMR Lapidary Equipment & Supplies, Pitlochry, Perthshire, Scotland
Rough and Tumble Ltd, 3 Tyne Street, North Shields, Northumberland
Scotrocks Partners, 48 Park Road, Glasgow C4, Scotland
Barbara Snelling, 349 Lymington Road, Highcliffe, Dorset
Sutherland Gemcutters, Achmelvich by Lairg, Sutherland, Scotland
Thompson & Beevers Limited, St. Just in Penwith, Cornwall
Tideswell Dale Rock Shop, Tideswell, Derbyshire
Wessex Gems and Crafts, Longacre, Downs Road, South Wonston,
    Winchester, Hants.

USA

Allcraft, 22 West 48th Street, New York, New York 10036
American Handicraft Company, Inc., 20 West 14th Street, New York, New
    York 10011
Anchor Tool and Supply Company, Inc., 12 John Street, New York, N.Y.
    10038
Anoziro Jewelers, 4002 North Stone Avenue, P.O. Box 3988, Tuscon, Ariz.
    85718
Baldwin-Taylor Hardware & Rock Shop, 4301 Jefferson Highway, New
    Orleans, Louisiana 70121
Diamond Pacific Tool Corporation, 24063 W. Main Street, Barstow, CA 92311
Geode Industries, 106–108 W. Main, Highway 34, New London, Iowa 52645
Geode Industries, Inc., 107 West Main Street, New London, Iowa 52645
Gilman's, Hellertown, PA. 18055
International Gem, 15 Maiden Lane, New York, New York 10038
Lapribrade Inc., 8 East Eagle Road, Havertown, Pennsylvania 19083
Lapidary Center, 4114 Judah Street, San Francisco, California 94122
Highland Park Manufacturing (Division of Musto Industries Inc.), 12600
    Chadron Avenue, Hawthorne, California 90250
Lortone Division of the Carborundum Company, Seattle, Washington 98107
MDR Manufacturing Co. Inc., 4853 Jefferson Blvd., Los Angeles, Cal. 90016

LAPIDARY SOCIETIES IN GREAT BRITAIN

Amateur Geological Society, Central Square, London NW11
Bath Mineral and Lapidary Society, Wiltshire
Berkshire Rockhounds, Reading, Berkshire
Blackpool Mineral and Lapidary Club, Blackpool, Lancashire
Bristol and District Lapidary Society, Bristol
Cambridge Lapidary Club
Cheltenham Mineral and Lapidary Club, Gloucestershire
Chorley Lapidary Club, Salop
Danum Lapidary Society, Doncaster, Yorkshire
Dartford Lapidary Society, Kent
Essex Rock and Mineral Society, Chelmsford, Essex
Falkirk Lapidary Club, Stirlingshire
Golspie Lapidary Club, Golspie, Sutherland
Kingston Lapidary Society, Kingston upon Hull, Yorkshire
Leeds Lapidary Society, Leeds, Yorkshire
London Gem and Rock Club, London
London Natural History Society, Geology Section, London E9
Medway Lapidary and Mineral Society
Natural History Society, London
Norfolk Mineral and Lapidary Society
North County Lapidary Society, Handforth, Cheshire
North West Lapidary Society, Cheadle, Cheshire
North Surrey Lapidary Society, Epsom, Surrey
Pentland Lapidary Society, Currie, Midlothian
Scottish Mineral and Lapidary Club, Edinburgh
Sutherlands Rockhounds, Dornoch, Sutherland
Teesside Lapidary Society, Middlesborough, Teesside
Thanet Mineral and Lapidary Society, Broadstairs, Kent
Warrington Lapidary Society, Warrington, Lancashire
Wessex Lapidary Society, Olivers Battery, Winchester
West of Scotland Mineral and Lapidary Society, Glasgow
Whitehaven and District Mineral and Lapidary Society, Whitehaven,
  Cumberland

The Gemmological Association of Great Britain runs courses for the
identification of gemstones and information on these courses may be obtained
from the Secretary of the Association, St Dunstan's House, Carey Lane,
London EC2.

The Geological Museum, Exhibition Road, London SW7 is also a useful source
of information.

INDEX

H3